History Heroes: Faith and Darkness

Short Stories by John X. Crabtree

Copyright 2024 by John X. Crabtree
Pending via the United States Copyright Office

All rights reserved.
No part of this book may be reproduced or transmitted by any means without permission of the author.

Library of Congress Cataloging-in-Publication Data

ISBN 979-8-218-57200-6

Contents

History Heroes: Faith and Darkness	4
Sam, You Are My Hero!	6
Thomas Jefferson, the Devil at Monticello	15
Legal Immigration Wanted!	24
John Quincy Adams, The Principled Patriot	26
Theodore Roosevelt, A Fighter for the Planet	32
Native Americans, Hoping for a Better Future	40
Robert F. Kennedy, the Compassionate Heart	43
Richard M. Nixon, Tricky Dick and the Chennault Affair	51
George Floyd, We Shall Overcome	63
Ronald Reagan, in Love with America	66
Admiral James Stockdale, a Stoic Mind	82
Technology, AI, and the Brave New World	91
Edward M. Kennedy, the Death of Dreams	95
Elvis Presley, a World without a King	107
The U.S. Debt, the Next Black Swan	119
Charlie Munger, Wisdom and Humor	122
Queen of Heaven	130
Forgiveness	133
Endnotes	134

History Heroes: Faith and Darkness

This book provides insightful knowledge through short stories about twelve interesting people in history. Each chapter is dedicated to an individual and their unique journey as it unfolded. I have tried to capture the essence of these famous people by drawing on defining aspects of their lives. I believe I was successful, but ultimately, that will be up to you to decide.

It is fascinating to study these individuals. Some performed well under intense pressure, while others self-destructed and plunged into the darkness. Several survived unthinkable circumstances, and one carried the weight of the world on her shoulders. Some are kind and believe in helping their fellow man, while others are contradictory, vindictive, and Machiavellian. A few struggled in the shadows of influential family members, while others failed to live up to the ideals they once championed.

One thing is certain: every event in history sets off a chain reaction leading us to where we are now. History can be messy; we like to think of our heroes as perfect, incapable of disappointing us, but we know that is not true. We hunger to relate to our heroes and sometimes wish we could go back in history and save them—from death and, in some cases, from themselves.

Writing is my special way of escaping my own mortality. A published book allows me to live forever on a bookshelf in a library or in the digital universe.

Lastly, and most importantly, a direct message to my two children: I want you both to know that your actions or inactions have consequences. Try to reach your full potential and continue to have intellectual curiosity as you pursue your passions. Make sure to have a voice. Standing up for what you believe in is necessary in this world. I'm always reminded of what Alexander Hamilton once said: "Those who stand for nothing fall for anything." Be firm in your beliefs and follow your own path. When hardships strike, and they will, seek support from your family and friends and professional help if you need it. The valleys of life can build character and in the long run, make you stronger, so continue to press forward.

I want you both to know that anything is possible if you set your minds to it. Enjoy your life—love, laugh.

Heartfelt wishes,

Dad

Sam, You Are My Hero!

Journalist and author Tom Brokaw popularized the term "the Greatest Generation." For those too young to remember, Brokaw was a fixture on the *NBC Nightly News* from 1982 to 2004. Brokaw found the perfect words to describe the men and women who served in World War II, both at home and abroad.

My grandfather, who was called "Sam," would have never considered himself great, that's for sure. He served his country in World War II without hesitation because that was simply what he was supposed to do.

My grandfather was born August 3, 1926, in Haverhill, Massachusetts. He grew up in the tough neighborhood of Ashland Street, a blue-collar area known for a handful of historic figures and a river that runs through it. Haverhill gave us historic figures such as Hannah Dustin, a Puritan woman who wielded an ax and scalped ten Native Americans as she and two others escaped their captors, the Abenaki, in 1697. During the ordeal, Hannah Dustin's newborn baby was killed, but she exacted her revenge, displaying the toughness of a frontier woman. A statue of Hannah Dustin with an ax is a fixture across the street from the Haverhill public library.[1]

Henry David Thoreau and his brother built a homemade wooden boat and set out on an expedition on the Merrimack River in August 1839, passing through Haverhill. This journey inspired Thoreau's first book, *A Week on the Concord and Merrimack Rivers*. Haverhill was also the birthplace of the famous abolitionist and writer John Greenleaf Whittier.

Additionally, Haverhill earned the nickname "Queen Slipper City" because it was a leader in the shoe industry.[2]

My grandfather entered the Navy at seventeen years old on August 13, 1943. To enlist at that age, he needed consent from his parents. His military bio reads:

Entered Navy August 13, 1943; discharged January 14, 1946. Seaman 1/c, USS Quincy. 9 months overseas. Service ribbons—European-African-Middle Eastern with 1 battle star; Asiatic-Pacific; American Theater. Principal location in U. S., Newport Training Station, Newport Rhode Island.

World War II, which lasted from 1939 to 1945, wreaked havoc across the globe. It was the deadliest war in history, involving thirty countries and resulting in an estimated eighty million deaths, including up to fifty-five million civilians. The Allies, which included France, Great Britain, the United States, the Soviet Union, and China, fought against the Axis powers, Germany, Italy, and Japan. Battles raged across Europe, Africa, and Asia, and of course at Pearl Harbor, which infuriated Americans. The President of the United States Franklin D. Roosevelt made an impassioned speech to defend freedom.[3]

> Mr. Vice President, Mr. Speaker, Members of the Senate, and of the House of Representatives:
> Yesterday, December 7th, 1941—a date which will live in infamy—the United States of America was suddenly and deliberately attacked by naval and air forces of the Empire of Japan.
> The United States was at peace with that nation and, at the solicitation of Japan, was still in conversation with its government and its emperor looking toward the maintenance of peace in the Pacific.

Indeed, one hour after Japanese air squadrons had commenced bombing in the American island of Oahu, the Japanese ambassador to the United States and his colleague delivered to our Secretary of State a formal reply to a recent American message. And while this reply stated that it seemed useless to continue the existing diplomatic negotiations, it contained no threat or hint of war or of armed attack.

It will be recorded that the distance of Hawaii from Japan makes it obvious that the attack was deliberately planned many days or even weeks ago. During the intervening time, the Japanese government has deliberately sought to deceive the United States by false statements and expressions of hope for continued peace.

The attack yesterday on the Hawaiian islands has caused severe damage to American naval and military forces. I regret to tell you that very many American lives have been lost. In addition, American ships have been reported torpedoed on the high seas between San Francisco and Honolulu.

Yesterday, the Japanese government also launched an attack against Malaya.

Last night, Japanese forces attacked Hong Kong.

Last night, Japanese forces attacked Guam.

Last night, Japanese forces attacked the Philippine Islands.

Last night, the Japanese attacked Wake Island.

And this morning, the Japanese attacked Midway Island.

Japan has, therefore, undertaken a surprise offensive extending throughout the Pacific area. The facts of yesterday and today speak for themselves. The people of the United States have already formed their opinions and well understand the implications to the very life and safety of our nation.

As Commander in Chief of the Army and Navy, I have directed that all measures be taken for our defense. But always will our whole nation remember the character of the onslaught against us.

No matter how long it may take us to overcome this premeditated invasion, the American people in their righteous might will win through to absolute victory.

I believe that I interpret the will of the Congress and of the people when I assert that we will not only defend ourselves to the uttermost, but will make it very certain that this form of treachery shall never again endanger us.

Hostilities exist. There is no blinking at the fact that our people, our territory, and our interests are in grave danger.

With confidence in our armed forces, with the unbounding determination of our people, we will gain the inevitable triumph—so help us God.

I ask that the Congress declare that since the unprovoked and dastardly attack by Japan on Sunday, December 7th, 1941, a state of war has existed between the United States and the Japanese empire.[4]

My grandmother said President Franklin D. Roosevelt's speech made a profound impact on my grandfather and motivated the greatest nation on earth to answer the call to arms and vanquish its enemies. You often hear the expression, "Youth is wasted on the young," but that certainly did not apply to this generation of young men and women. They went away to fight a war as boys, and they returned as men. This was especially true for my grandfather, who was only seventeen when he entered the war. My grandfather embarked on the adventure of a lifetime, but at what cost to his mental health?

My grandfather's service on the USS *Quincy* (CA-71) proved to be historically significant for several reasons. The USS *Quincy* supported troops by providing heavy gunfire during the D-Day invasion on June 6, 1944, at Utah Beach. His ship then went on the offensive, bombarding the Germans in Cherbourg, France. Later in August 1944, the *Quincy* provided gunfire support during the invasion of Southern France.

If that wasn't historic enough, my grandfather must have been thrilled when the President who had inspired him to serve traveled on his ship. In

February 1945, the USS *Quincy* transported President Franklin D. Roosevelt to the Yalta conference from Newport News, Virginia, to Malta. The President then used air transport to attend the historic conference, which famously hosted the "Big Three"—Winston Churchill, Joseph Stalin, and President Roosevelt.

The *Quincy* was also the site of other historic meetings involving President Franklin Roosevelt. Emperor Selassie of Ethiopia, King Farouk of Egypt, and King Abdul Aziz Ibn Saud of Saudi Arabia all sat aboard *Quincy* to discuss the war. Later, the *Quincy* escorted aircraft carriers as the United States conducted airstrikes on the Japanese home islands. When the Japanese surrendered, the *Quincy* was involved in occupation efforts.[5]

People often say, "You never know what is going on inside someone's head." They could be suffering from health problems, the loss of a spouse, or, as in the case of my grandfather, war- related issues. My grandfather was a part of the Greatest Generation, but after the war, he certainly didn't feel special. He was a silent sufferer, and it is safe to say he was a self-medicating with alcohol. He gambled and often became reclusive. The Greatest Generation never complained; they just moved forward the best they could with what they had.

As they say, great minds discuss ideas, average minds discuss events, small minds discuss people. My grandfather was a tough nut to crack because he hardly discussed anything at all, but there were some clues in life that gave some of him away.

My grandfather never owned a car, and he walked or took public transportation everywhere except for work, where his brother would give him a ride because they were employed at Western Electric. He seldom ever showed emotion to me but did give me advice: "Slow horses and fast women will kill you every time." He always gave me a dollar from a roll of money that was in his shirt pocket, which, looking back, I realize he probably made from gambling.

My grandfather didn't have much of a relationship with my grandmother, who was a saint. She once told me, "He was much different before the war." She cooked and cleaned for him, but there was no great affection between them. They were more like roommates who got along to a point. For the Greatest Generation, the thought of divorce was out of the question; it was taboo back then, much different than today. My grandfather would make a quick appearance at the holidays and then slip quietly out the backdoor, or sometimes he wouldn't even show up, which became more common as I got older. You wonder if the effects of being in a war at such a young age caused him a lifetime of mental issues that he couldn't quite get his arms around.

As a veteran, my grandfather qualified for military housing, but in retrospect there was nothing special about it. These apartments had heavy doors and a cement floor that was always cool in summer and ice cold in the winter. I remember going there as a kid, holding onto the iron railings and walking two flights of stairs to their apartment door. I recall my grandmother always cooking something that you could smell down the staircase as soon as you stepped into the hallway. They had a dog named Dixie that was stationed under the table just in case food fell on the ground. The problem is that if you moved your feet too quickly under the table, your socks were ripped off your feet and Dixie might take a nip at one of your toes in the process.

Looking back, I realize they struggled to make ends meet. Their small apartment housed three children in only two bedrooms. It was very small, a little bigger than a studio apartment. You would have thought that heroes deserved more, but my grandfather's plight was no different than that of many others who served our country.

When the last child moved out in the early 1980s, my grandfather took the spare room for himself. It was transformed into a small man cave that always smelled like a Camel unfiltered, his choice of smokes. His coffee table was covered in beer bottles, with the newspaper opened up to the box scores of baseball games near an ashtray filled with cigarette butts. His favorite hat, a tweed fedora, hung on the back of the door. In the left corner of his room, he had a small closet and a half-length mirror next to a small dresser and a pull-out couch. Scotch-taped to the mirror was a poem called "The Man in the Glass" by Dale Wimbrow, written in 1934.

The Man in the Glass

When you get what you want in your struggle for self
And the world makes you king for a day
Just go to the mirror and look at yourself
And see what that man has to say.

For it isn't your father, or mother, or wife
Whose judgment upon you must pass
The fellow whose verdict counts most in your life
Is the one staring back from the glass.

He's the fellow to please—never mind all the rest
For he's with you, clear to the end
And you've passed your most difficult, dangerous test
If the man in the glass is your friend.

You may fool the whole world down the pathway of years
And get pats on the back as you pass
But your final reward will be heartache and tears
If you've cheated the man in the glass.

I realized that "The Man in the Glass" was my grandfather, who suffered mentally and needed professional help but never got it. He fell into the same negative patterns repeatedly. I came to learn that the vets of World War II did not receive help for post-traumatic stress disorder (PTSD). The simple reason is that PTSD was not recognized as a medical problem until 1980. Terms such as "combat fatigue" or "shell shock" were used to describe World War II vets' mental issues. I didn't understand him at all back then, but today, I think I can piece some of it together. Still, he remains somewhat of a mystery.[6]

When I look in the mirror and wonder if I am doing my best, I realize reflecting on who you are truthfully can be difficult, but it's a necessary step in our personal growth and self-improvement. We all have fallen short in our life at some point, and it might be agonizing to look that deep within. My grandfather probably read "The Man in the Glass" each morning after drinking too much or losing a bet, and perhaps he vowed to change, but he never did. His story ended with his death on May 16, 1990, a few months after he retired from Western Electric at 63. He never got to enjoy his old age and sadly never figured himself out. Today, we have many resources for people, especially vets, that can support them in their time of need.

As for my grandfather, I wish I could go back in time and let him know that I thought "The Man in the Glass" was a history hero.

Thomas Jefferson, the Devil at Monticello

For a fleeting moment in history, America could be viewed as the "New Eden," a nation born free. The Declaration of Independence declared, "We hold these truths to be self-evident, that all men are created equal, that they are endowed by their Creator with certain unalienable Rights, that among these are Life, Liberty and the pursuit of Happiness." Thomas Jefferson's words captured the true meaning of what it meant to be a citizen of this brave new nation.

Brimming with hope and promise, the Declaration became one of the most celebrated documents of American history, perhaps even worldwide. Its impact inspired numerous regional and nationalist groups to declare in writing their own desire for separation from their oppressors.

The Declaration sparked debate and led men and women to fight for their rights. But to whom did the document refer when it said, "all men"? What exactly were "certain unalienable rights"? Thomas Jefferson owned slaves and had an intimate relationship with one, who in consequence bore his children. Can we still celebrate a document penned by a slaveholder? Can we reconcile ourselves with Jefferson's hypocrisy, his crimes?

Jefferson's contemporary, John Adams, reminds us that not all the founding fathers shared Jefferson's views on slavery. "Every measure of prudence, therefore, ought to be assumed for the eventual total extirpation of slavery from the United States," he wrote. "I have, throughout my whole life, held the practice of slavery in abhorrence."

It is curious that the two ran against each other twice for president, Adams winning in 1796 and Jefferson, who was Adams' vice president at the time, triumphing in the election of 1800. You might think owning slaves, especially as the author of the Declaration of Independence, would be a deal-breaker and would have cost him the presidency. Unfortunately, slavery was accepted at the time in the South, where several other influential leaders were also slaveowners. The issues of the election centered on foreign policy, states' rights, and the federal government's role in America, not slavery.[7]

The Adams family understood the true meaning of independence. John Adams' son, John Quincy Adams, who became the sixth president of the United States and then a congressman, later said slavery is "A sin before the sight of God."[8]

But unfortunately, the underlying message during this time was that the Declaration of Independence wasn't written for people of color or women—it was intended for rich white men. Thomas Jefferson interpreted it in a way that best worked for him.[9]

When I review Jefferson's track record, I almost want to scream—Why? Your Declaration of Independence was written perfectly, and your presidential accomplishments were outstanding! How could you be so shortsighted?

There are likely many answers to this question that will never make sense to me. If you were the author of arguably the most transformative document in history, why wouldn't you strive to live up to it? Would you do the opposite of what you wrote and commit egregious crimes against humanity? Engaging in this mental exercise is mind-numbing because Jefferson was smart enough to know better.

So when I read about his accomplishments, it is disappointing beyond words. Jefferson could have been ranked by historians as the number one president of all time. His legacy includes significant contributions to the founding and expansion of the United States.[10]

Author of the Declaration of Independence (1776)

Studied law at the College of William and Mary in (1763)

Governor of Virginia from (1779–1781)

U.S. Minister of France (1785–1789)

First Secretary of State under President Washington (1790–1793)

Second Vice President of The United States (1789–1801

Third President of the United States (1801–1809)

As President, doubled the size of the U.S. with the Louisiana Purchase (1803)

Founder of the University of Virginia (1819)

As ex-president, sold his library to the U.S. government after the British set fire to the White House and burned other government buildings to the ground during the War of 1812, thus helping rebuild the Library of Congress.[11]

President Thomas Jefferson is a perfect example of the complex relationship that America has with race. When we peel back Jefferson's layers, what we find is quite disturbing.

Indeed, he had significant political accomplishments along with a successful educational background. He mastered several languages, including Latin, Greek, French, Spanish, Italian, and Anglo-Saxon. Jefferson was also an inventor, creating the revolving book stand, the dumbwaiter, cipher wheel, swivel chair, and moldboard plow. Monticello showcases Jefferson's impressive skills as an architect. The gardens at Monticello were immaculately kept and inspired by his travels to Europe. Unfortunately, both the home and garden were built with enslaved labor.[12]

In my view, Monticello is ground zero for the second greatest fall of man. Jefferson's relationship with his slave Sally Hemings has been scrutinized. He began his liaison with Hemings after his wife's death, and they had six children together, four of whom survived to adulthood. The idea of having an intimate relationship with a slave is inherently wrong, raising the question about power dynamics. This underscores the point that Thomas Jefferson was a very flawed individual, if not outright evil.[13]

The emotional and physical abuse of African Americans who were treated as property instead of as humans is incomprehensible. Women were raped and sometimes impregnated by their slave masters, and families were torn apart and sold, never to reunite. Some slaves were murdered or beaten nearly to death. Was this hell on Earth?

Did Jefferson consider the prospect of judgment in the afterlife? This is debatable given that his belief system rejected formal Christian religion and focused on the natural world. Historians have linked his views to Deism. Jefferson seemed to cherry pick the parts of Christianity that aligned with his views, believing that the message of Jesus was corrupted by the apostle Paul, Gospel writers, and the Protestant reformers.[14]

If you are a Christian, you might imagine Jefferson suffering in the fiery pits of hell for the pain he caused as a slave owner. By all accounts, he never sought forgiveness. Obviously, Jefferson thought it would be "Better to reign in hell, than to serve in heaven." Jefferson stated that slavery was a moral depravity and hideous blot, but his actions speak louder than his words. Throughout his life, he owned 600 slaves.

The line "Better to reign in Hell, than serve in Heaven" is from John Milton's epic poem *Paradise Lost*.[15]

Jefferson offered one pathetic excuse after another about how America should handle slavery in the future. Unsurprisingly, none of these solutions would affect him. It is the classic case of "Do as I say, not as I do."

Jefferson believed that the plantation's economy depended on slave labor. If the slaves were emancipated, what would become of his beloved Monticello? Money was a driving force for Jefferson, but it also presented a significant problem for him.

As Jon Meacham writes in *Thomas Jefferson: The Art of Power*, "Personal debt was another enduring irony of Jefferson's life. Planters of his time and place were often land rich and cash poor, borrowing heavily against their farms, their slaves and their prospective crops." Meacham adds, "A confluence of factors kept Jefferson in debt. There was the gentry culture of his time. Of course, Jefferson had to live up to his social status and spending lavishly on unnecessary things was a part of the deal."

Meacham profoundly writes, "Why would Jefferson, a man who sought power over men and events, concede his power to creditors and continue to incur debts when he was already so burdened." Jefferson's death in 1826 resulted in the loss of Monticello to debt.[16]

Jefferson also believed that gradually freeing the slaves was the solution. Naturally, this would not affect him at all since these actions would take place long after his death. He thought immediate emancipation would lead to unrest or chaos in the nation. Jefferson described his true feelings on slavery in a letter to John Holmes on April 22, 1820: "But, as it is, we have the wolf by the ear, and we can neither hold him, nor safely let him go."[17]

Jefferson believed that African Americans were inferior to Whites. He also claimed that slaves were better off under the care of their masters, which is just another twisted excuse to continue with the status quo.[18]

Slavery reached its peak by 1860, with four million being held in bondage in the South, where King Cotton reigned supreme. The wickedness of slavery left a permanent scar on America, and the man who wrote arguably the greatest document on Earth saw his reputation forever tarnished. Jefferson came to embody the image of a lying, self-serving politician—one who is chastised and scoffed at for believing in nothing but himself and caring only about lining his own pockets.[19] Moncure Daniel Conway, an abolitionist and a co-editor of an anti-slavery paper,

The Commonwealth, once remarked about Thomas Jefferson, "Never did a man achieve more fame for what he did not do."[20]

Many continue to make excuses for Jefferson in an attempt to compartmentalize his actions, separating the parts we like from the parts we don't. This technique of filtering out his moral failures are common. At a dinner party at the White House in 1962 for Nobel Prize winners, President John Kennedy said, "I think this is the most extraordinary collection of talent, of human knowledge, that has ever been gathered together at the White House, with the possible exception of when Thomas Jefferson dined alone."[21]

Of course, Kennedy was avoiding the obvious, and it would not have been appropriate to criticize Jefferson's slave ownership during a White House dinner. But one has to wonder why Kennedy would pay Jefferson a compliment on his intellectual prowess, knowing his grave faults. The short answer is that it is easier to present our founding fathers as geniuses, as men without moral flaws who knew what was best for the country. The sin of slavery certainly diminishes the principles of freedom, equality, and justice that our country was founded upon, and at the same time, it diminishes Jefferson. A deeper answer might be that adopting the myth creates a perception of who our forefathers ought to have been instead of who they really were.

Kennedy gave a national address on Civil Rights on June 11, 1963, highlighting segregation in public schools and the violence and obstruction that occurred at the University of Alabama. A portion of

President Kennedy's speech regarding equality and opportunities in America particularly struck me:

> It ought to be possible, therefore, for American students of any color to attend any public institution they select without having to be backed up by troops. It ought to be possible for American consumers of any color to receive equal services in places of public accommodations, such as hotels and restaurants and theaters and retail stores, without being forced to resort to demonstrations in the street, and it ought to be possible for American citizens of any color to register and to vote in a free election without interference or fear of reprisal. It ought to be possible, in short, for every American to enjoy the privileges of being American without regard to his race or his color.[22]

I wonder if President Kennedy ever thought Jefferson really dropped the ball on freedom after writing such a beautiful document, the Declaration of Independence. Did he ever think that Jefferson's actions and bad behavior contributed to poor race relations in America?

There is a reason President Obama placed his left hand on two Bibles when he took the oath of office. The Bibles belonged to President Lincoln and Dr. Martin Luther King, Jr. Obama recognized that he stood on the shoulders of history, and he paid homage to their greatness. Obama's presidency reminded America how far we have come since our original sin of slavery. On the one hand, Obama's presidency can be seen as proof that the Declaration of Independence finally worked, but on the other, it raised questions of why it took so long.

Jefferson's sins had damning consequences not only in his time, but also in present-day America. Race riots and murders have plagued our country since its founding.

Jefferson's sin spread to all aspects of society, creating hate and discontent between races, genders, and sexualities. Discrimination and prejudice rear their ugly heads from time to time in both large cities and small towns across America.

Although it is debatable whether Jefferson can be forgiven, his Declaration of Independence miraculously continues to shape our country's future, and his words still inspire liberty and democracy around the world, even if his private life and ownership of slaves were controversial. We still aim to live out the true meaning of the Declaration, but in our hearts, we know it will forever be just out of reach. One can view Jefferson's Declaration of Independence as his saving grace, while others might think of him as the Devil at Monticello.

Legal Immigration Wanted!

America is the best country on the planet, and understandably, immigrants are willing to risk their lives to get here. Considering the current situation in countries south of our border, which have high crime rates and poor economies, I can understand their people's desire for a better life here in America.

When undocumented migrants enter our country illegally, they are often exploited for cheap labor in jobs that most Americans will not take: picking fruits and vegetables, roofing houses, general labor, janitorial work, housekeeping, factory work, and serving as nannies. These jobs frequently come with no health-care benefits. So we must shut off that magnet, and businesses should abide by the laws. We can't claim to be against illegal immigration while simultaneously providing them with jobs when they get here.

I also understand that safety concerns arise when we don't know who is entering our country. Consider, for example, the death of Laken Riley, a twenty-two-year-old nursing student at Augusta University, who was murdered by Jose Antonio Ibarra, a twenty-six-year-old from Venezuela who crossed the border into America illegally. Laken Riley was jogging in a wooded area near Lake Herrick. An autopsy documented injuries to her head, neck, torso, and limbs. A rock most likely caused her skull fracture. Ibarra intended to rape her but murdered her before he could. He was sentenced to life in prison with no chance of parole.[23]

Laken would have become a nurse someday, helping others, but instead she was murdered. We need an immigration system that works, keeping drugs and unwanted criminals, like murderers and the cartels, out of our country. The world has to know that we are a country of laws and borders.

We want legal immigration and to continue celebrating diversity in this nation. Think about your ancestors who, for a variety of reasons, came to America—escaping poverty, or war, or religious persecution. These men and women helped build this country, raised their families here, and chased down the American dream.

I'm reminded of the words of Emma Lazarus, a Jewish American poet. She inspired a nation that is rich in diversity and full of opportunity. She wrote "The New Colossus" in 1883 and it was inscribed on a bronze plaque on the Statue of Liberty in 1903.

The New Colossus
Not like the brazen giant of Greek fame
With conquering limbs astride from land to land;
Here at our sea-washed, sunset gates shall stand
A mighty woman with a torch, whose flame
Is the imprisoned lightning, and her name
Mother of Exiles. From her beacon-hand
Glows world-wide welcome; her mild eyes command
The air-bridged harbor that twin cities frame,
"Keep, ancient lands, your storied pomp!" cries she
With silent lips. "Give me your tired, your poor,
Your huddled masses yearning to breathe free,
The wretched refuse of your teeming shore,
Send these, the homeless, tempest-tossed to me,
I lift my lamp beside the golden door!"[24]

John Quincy Adams, The Principled Patriot

From time to time, we all need counsel about life's tricky decisions. Having a trusted role model can be very helpful. Rather than focusing solely on the end result, it's essential to emphasize the journey toward realizing one's dreams. There's wisdom in listening to those who are older and have more experience. If we can listen to our elders, perhaps we can avoid some costly mistakes.

John Quincy Adams had guidance from his parents. The Adams family set an example that prioritized public service over material wealth. John and Abigail Adams were attentive parents who made sure that their children were well cared for, which certainly included education. John Quincy Adams had no choice but to be brilliant. He got first-hand experience of American history from his parents, who worked tirelessly to forge a new nation. The American Revolution was fought against the number one superpower on Earth, Great Britain. The British of course had made their mark on the world by imposing their dominance through military superiority. It was often said that the sun never set on the British Empire.

When his father, the "Colossus of Independence," John Adams, died at age of ninety on July 4, 1826—ironically, the fiftieth anniversary of the Declaration of Independence—the world came to a halt for his son John Quincy Adams, who was at the time was the sixth president of the United States. When he returned home, he had much to reflect on regarding the loss of his father, but also the loss of another former president and founding father, Thomas Jefferson. The two had died only hours apart.

John Adams and Thomas Jefferson had faced off in two epic presidential elections, with each claiming one victory. John Adams won the first contest in 1796, in which Jefferson became the vice president. Jefferson won the rematch in 1800 in a truly an ugly contest that revealed the disturbingly cutthroat nature of politics. The election of 1800 severed their relationship, and the two did not communicate for 12 years.[25]

At the suggestion of Benjamin Rush, Adams was the first to reach out to Jefferson. The two exchanged letters from 1812 until their deaths in 1826. These letters record what these two giants of history were thinking about. The topics ranged from religion to politics to policies, and, of course, to personal losses. Their letters also provided valuable insights into the birth of a nation.[26]

Now that these two giants were gone, Americans reflected on their accomplishments and their finest hours in creating and then leading the best country on Earth. In honor of his father and Thomas Jefferson, President John Quincy Adams issued an executive order to lower the U.S. flags to half-staff.[27]

John Quincy's diary proved to be a window into his soul. He wrote, "That moment to me was inexpressibly painful and struck as if it had been an arrow to the heart." He did not attend his father's funeral because he did not find out the older Adams had died until more than a week later. At that time, instant communication did not exist. Samuel Morse did not invent the telegraph until 1844. It could take weeks or longer for letters to be delivered to and from Massachusetts and Washington, D.C., depending on weather and road conditions.[28]

His mother Abigail was not there to console her son; she died in 1818 of typhoid fever at the age of seventy-three, never seeing her son become president.[29] John Quincy Adams was now without both his beloved parents. He went on to fulfill the family legacy of public service, leaving his most significant mark as a congressman from Massachusetts.

John Quincy Adams had strong connections through his father, but also the smarts to carry out these political appointments and shine on the world stage. He served as United States Minister to the Netherlands during George Washington's administration; United States Minister to Prussia during his father's tenure as president; United States Minister to Russia, playing a crucial role in diplomatic negotiations in St. Petersburg; United States Minister to the United Kingdom; eighth United States Secretary of State (1817–1825); sixth President of the United States (1825–1829); member of the U.S. House of Representatives from Massachusetts (1831–1848); and fourteenth Dean of the United States House of Representatives (1844–1848).[30]

Like his father, John Quincy Adams had no patience for compromise. He was stubborn and had difficulty persuading politicians to get what he wanted. John Quincy Adams was certainly not a backroom deal-cutter. He was a man with firm beliefs. Unfortunately, politics and making deals are part of being a successful president. John Adams stressed early on to his son the example of Cicero, the Roman statesman and philosopher. John Adams believed that making enemies in politics might indicate you are doing something right. Cicero succumbed to his enemies eventually, but not without making a lasting impact on the importance of moral virtue. John Quincy followed the Cicero approach as he served the nation in his various political offices.[31]

The election of John Quincy Adams in 1824 to the presidency was controversial because none of the candidates won a majority of electoral votes. All the candidates—Andrew Jackson, Henry Clay, William Crawford, and John Quincy Adams—were from the Democratic Republican Party. The House of Representatives determined the election because none of the candidates won a majority of the electoral votes. John Quincy Adams won the presidency, but it cost him much political capital.

During John Quincy Adams' presidency, he was met with fierce headwinds and didn't have the political clout in Congress to achieve his main initiatives, which were internal improvements to the country. Adams sought to create infrastructure projects, scientific advancements, and educational reforms. He did receive support for the Cumberland Road and did secure funding for the Smithsonian Institution, but overall, his much larger proposals were dead in the water. Like his father before him, John Quincy Adams became a one term-president. Many thought his political obituary was written, and most thought he would retire to the garden, as his father had. No one expected that the former president would resurface as a congressmen and serve eighteen years, actually dying on the floor of the House of Representatives. I feel his service in Congress defines his career and places him in the upper echelon of public servants.[32]

The two issues that solidified John Quincy Adams as a man of integrity were his opposition to the Gag Rule and the Amistad Case. The Gag Rule was a legislative tactic created in 1830 that banned any comment or discussion of slavery in the country. Despite the prospect of censure, Adams succeeded in allowing open debate on this moral issue. He faced fierce opposition attacks and even death threats, but Adams persisted in opposing enslavement with speech after speech. Eventually, the Gag Rule was rescinded in December 1844.[33]

The Amistad Case became yet another defining feather in John Quincy's cap. In 1839, the enslaved Africans being transported on the *Amistad*, a Spanish slave ship, overcame their captors and seized the ship off the coast of Cuba. John Quincy took the case before the Supreme Court. He made a passionate defense, citing the founders but, most importantly the Declaration of Independence, which by all accounts convinced the Supreme Court to issue a 7-1 ruling on March 9, 1841. African Americans had been illegally enslaved and have every right to fight for their freedom. It was a fitting victory for a man whose father was the only founding father on record to not hold slaves and who, along with his wife Abigail, believed that slavery was evil. Their Puritan faith of goodness and moral erectness thrived in their son John Quincy Adams, who made a defense for the ages.

John Quincy was infused with character traits such as integrity and a sense of justice from his parents. His actions changed history for the better.

Theodore Roosevelt, A Fighter for the Planet

The year is 2099, and a small seacoast town in Maine on the mouth of the ocean has been swallowed whole by Mother Nature. Sea water has filled the streets over a foot deep. Water rushes into a resort where happy vacationers once left their worries behind for a relaxing stay. The wind whistles, and your eyes sting, tears stream down your face; a burning smell almost suffocates you. The temperature is nearly 80 degrees, and it's February.

Fires in neighboring communities can be seen in the distance, and boats once docked in the harbor have washed up in the street and in the local grocery store's parking lot. Many of the red bricks that made up the beautiful sidewalk in front of the post office have gone missing, swept away into the ocean. One gold-framed picture of a Red Dazzler canna lily hangs in an abandoned art gallery window. Was it left on purpose or forgotten when the owners evacuated years ago? One thing is for sure—this once joyous community will eventually find a permanent resting place beneath the sea.

Curfews are set each night throughout the country because of violence and looting. Various health issues arise, and the local pharmacies are out of business nationwide because they were ransacked years ago when there was a shortage of medicines. American citizens are now dependent on the government for their supplies. The security of nuclear missiles is a concern not just in America, but elsewhere in the world.

Those who have survived all these crises wonder why the generations before them failed to act, failed to lead. Did they not care about the future and the people and wildlife in it? Were they self-absorbed, more focused on sharing trivial content on Facebook and Instagram? Were they ensnared by their technology, seemingly devoid of empathy?

This is one of many dark climate change scenarios that we can escape only if we work together!

The challenge not only lies with the government doing the right thing, but also in galvanizing citizens' efforts. Can we rise above self-interest, politics, and economic concerns? Can we find a leader who can unify the country and the world, because today we simply don't have it on either side of the political aisle? Can we find a leader who exhibits such qualities of passion and concern for our environment? If we could only bring back to life our twenty-sixth president, Theodore Roosevelt.

You wonder how Theodore Roosevelt might fare in this day and age with the mainstream press and social media. Would he run wild with his bully pulpit, changing hearts and minds on the issue of climate change? Would his messaging break the internet? Would he call out fake news? Roosevelt had a fearless reputation in war as a Rough Rider and in politics as a trustbuster, but he also won a Nobel Peace Prize and negotiated a treaty with Panama that gave the United States the right to build a canal that connected the Pacific and Atlantic Oceans. Roosevelt was the first President in 1906 to leave the United States to travel abroad to visit the construction site of the canal. Roosevelt had endless energy and excellent political instincts.[34]

Theodore Roosevelt was a Harvard graduate who majored in American history and government. He enrolled in Columbia University Law School, but did not complete the program. Roosevelt was more interested in politics. At the age of twenty-three, he was elected to the New York state assembly. He was called the "cyclone assembly man" by the press because of his intense energy.

February 14, 1884, was no doubt a defining point in Theodore Roosevelt's life. On that day, his wife, Alice Lee Roosevelt, died of a kidney ailment. She was only twenty-two. She had just given birth to their daughter Alice two days before. Unbelievably, his mother, Mittie Roosevelt, died on the same day of typhoid fever at fifty years of age. The emotional devastation of these losses sent Theodore Roosevelt's life off on a different path. He sought refuge in the Badlands in the Dakota territory and relied on his sister Bamie to attend to his infant daughter. Roosevelt spent two years as a rancher and sheriff and invested most of his free time reading and writing. He embraced cowboy life and brought his own personal style to the West with his sombrero, six-shooter, a Tiffany knife, fringed buckskin clothing, and spurs. In a sense, the rebirth of Theodore Roosevelt in the Badlands propelled him to new heights of success. He famously said he would not have been president had it not been for his experiences in North Dakota.[35]

Roosevelt explored this country and understood what made America tick. He encapsulated the American dream and took on life full throttle with grit and self-determination. This paid off dividends for Roosevelt, because unlike most Ivy League politicians, Roosevelt became a man of the people.

Roosevelt's resume shows how he climbed the ladder to success.

U.S. Civil Service Commission (1889–1895)

New York City Board of Police Commissioners (1895–1896)

Assistant Secretary of the Navy (1897–1898)

Colonel of the Rough Riders (1898)

Governor of New York (1899–1900)

Vice President of the United States (1901–1909)

Twenty-sixth President of the United States (1901–1909)

Winner of the Nobel Peace Prize in 1906 for having negotiated peace in the Russo-Japanese war in 1904–5

President of the American Historical Association (1912)

Founder of the Progressive Party (1912)

After taking over as President when William McKinley was assassinated, Theodore Roosevelt became the youngest to ever serve as president at forty-two years of age. John F. Kennedy was the youngest ever elected at forty-three, which is an important distinction. Roosevelt used his bully pulpit and made his case for conservation.

When Roosevelt was president, he created some of our most treasured national parks, including the Grand Canyon and Yosemite. He wanted to make sure these precious parts of America would always be protected. What President Roosevelt didn't realize that his conservation efforts would serve as carbon sinks that would store carbon emissions and help temper climate change.[36]

Here are some of Theodore Roosevelt's notable accomplishments.

Roosevelt established 150 national forests across the United States. He created the United States Forest Service (USFS) to manage and protect the nation's forests. This action ensured the conservation of timber and other natural resources, but it also will aid carbon sequestration, which is important in the fight against climate change. The forests roughly cover 30% of the land surface of the Earth. Trees absorb carbon dioxide and store it in wood, plant matter, and soil. Carbon would remain in our atmosphere if it wasn't for forests and the role they play in our ecosystem. Each year, the forests help remove two billion metric tons of carbon from the atmosphere. Roosevelt eventually protected up to 230 million acres of public lands.[37]

President Roosevelt worked with the legislative branch to establish these beautiful national parks:

Crater Lake National Park in Oregon in 1902

Wind Cave National Park in South Dakota in 1903

Sullys Hill in North Dakota 1904 (now managed by USFWS)

Platt National Park in Oklahoma in 1906 (now part of Chickasaw National Recreation Area)

Mesa Verde National Park in Colorado in 1906

Added the Mariposa Grove and Giant Sequoia Groves to Yosemite National Park in California in 1906.

On June 8, 1906, Theodore Roosevelt signed the National Monuments Act, which allows the president the discretion to "declare by public proclamation historic landmarks, to be National Monuments." Roosevelt did not need congressional approval to do this, so it was much easier to establish these national monuments than national parks. He dedicated the following sites as national monuments:

Devil's Tower in Wyoming in 1906

El Morro in New Mexico in 1906

Montezuma Castle in Arizona in 1906

Petrified Forest in Arizona in 1906 (now a national park)

Chaco Canyon in New Mexico in 1907

Lassen Peak in California in 1907 (now Lassen Volcanic National Park)

Cinder Cone in California in 1907 (now part of Lassen Volcanic National Park)

Gila Cliff Dwellings in New Mexico in 1907

Tonto in Arizona in 1907

Muir Woods in California in 1908

Grand Canyon in Arizona in 1908 (now a national park)

Pinnacles in California in 1908 (now a national park)

Jewel Cave in South Dakota in 1908

Natural Bridges in Utah in 1908

Lewis & Clark Caverns in Montana in 1908 (now a Montana state park)

Tumacácori in Arizona in 1908

Wheeler in Colorado in 1908 (now Wheeler Geologic Area, part of Rio Grande National Forest)

Mount Olympus in Washington in 1909 (now Olympic National Park)

Chalmette Monument and Grounds in 1907, a site of the Battle of New Orleans (now part Jean Lafitte National Historical Park)

President Roosevelt's wildlife conservation consisted of protecting four national game reserves and fifty-one federal bird reserves to safeguard bird populations and their dwellings. He also helped with the protection of bighorn sheep, elk, and deer.[38]

Toughness in this climate debate is needed. Theodore Roosevelt was so tough that he once gave a ninety-minute speech despite having been shot. On October 14, 1912, while campaigning for a third presidential term as a third-party candidate for the Progressive Party (also known as the Bull Moose Party), in Milwaukee, Roosevelt stood up in an open-air automobile and waved to the crowd, and was shot by John Schrank, a saloonkeeper. Luckily for Roosevelt, the bullet struck a steel eyeglass case in his coat pocket. Roosevelt insisted on making his speech, which he titled "Progressive Cause." Afterward, Roosevelt agreed to visit the hospital and later proclaimed, "I do not care a rap about being shot; not a rap." He lost his bid for reelection in a three-way race against the current president, William Howard Taft. Wilson prevailed, but history noted Roosevelt's fearlessness.

Theodore Roosevelt gave a speech at the Sorbonne in Paris, France, on April 23, 1910, that sums up his tenaciousness in the political arena.

> It is not the critic who counts, not the one who points out how the strong man stumbled or how the doer of deeds might have done them better. The credit belongs to the man who is actually in the arena, whose face is marred with sweat and dust and blood; who strives valiantly; who errs and comes short again and again; who knows the great enthusiasms, the great devotions, and spends himself in a worthy cause; who, if he wins, knows the triumph of high achievement; and who, if he fails, at least fails while daring greatly, so that his place shall never be with those cold and timid souls who know neither victory nor defeat.

Theodore Roosevelt solidified his legacy as a conservationist. He did not know that his efforts in the years between 1901 and 1909 would make him a modern-day climate change warrior. What will you do to save the planet? How can you get involved? Perhaps we need to reflect on our personal responsibility as stewards of the climate and environment. Perhaps the answers rest with us and not with some movie star or politician.

Maybe we can be the change!

Native Americans, Hoping for a Better Future

You can only imagine what was going through Native Americans' minds in 1492 when Christopher Columbus arrived in the Caribbean. When the local people, the Tainos, greeted him, Columbus called them "Indians." His voyages changed history, especially for the original inhabitants. Columbus, until the day he died in 1506, thought he had explored parts of Asia. In America, adventurers and white settlers followed him, forcing Native Americans out of their lands.[39]

Imagine being a Native American, standing on your land, watching these massive ships and men with metal objects arrive. The foreigners show up and steal land that isn't theirs. The white man puts a fence around the land and claims it belongs to them now. The Native Americans are confused because the white settlers don't own that. It's territory where they hunt and fish. This problem continued throughout Native American history. The Native Americans eventually lost almost everything and were forced onto reservations, where life can be difficult.

Looking back at our history, deception and disrespect have been common actions against Native Americans. Over time, the ugliness emerged, and we see killing, displacement, and spreading of deadly disease by white settlers. We also see attempts to assimilate and strip Native Americans of their heritage and culture. A disgusting example of this occurred at Harvard Indian College in Cambridge, Massachusetts, which was established in 1640. Students' long hair, which was a sign of strength for Native Americans, was cut, and they were forced to adopt English dress and convert to Christianity.

The United States signed 368 treaties with Native Americans and then systematically broke them.[40] Sitting Bull summed it up best: "What treaty have the Sioux made with the white man that we have broken? Not one. What treaty have the white man ever made with us that they have kept? Not one."[41]

I remember as a little boy I was fascinated with the crying Indian commercial.[42] Over time, I realized that the ad was fraudulent on many levels. For one, Iron Eyes Cody was actually Espera Oscar de Corti, an Italian-American, and the companies that were backing this ad didn't give a hoot about pollution. I also recall going to the grocery store and wanting the Cowboy and Indian Colorforms. These were vinyl cut-outs that you could place on a background of the Old West. You could design your picture using a variety of guns, bow and arrows, Indians and cowboys, wagons, and tepees.[43]

Growing up, I watched cowboy movies that depicted Native Americans as savages, with clear lines drawn between the good guys and bad guys. Over time, Hollywood began to recognize Native Americans and their struggles. Movies like *Dances with Wolves* starring Kevin Costner or *Last of the Mohicans* resonated by portraying Native Americans trying to hang onto their customs and their land.

My generation, and most definitely the ones before me, were conditioned to see only one side of the story. As I got older, I realized Native Americans were the victims.

The question is, how do we help the Native America today? We can make cuts to the federal government and then allocate more to the Bureau of Indian Affairs (BIA), which is part of the U.S. Department of the Interior. For the fiscal year 2024, the BIA's budget is $3.0 billion.

Maybe with cuts from the federal government, we can up the ante and target critical needs to the 326 recognized Native American reservations in the United States.[44] Each reservation is different with their own sets of problems, but an increase in funding can potentially help with education, cultural preservation, and health and human services and perhaps stimulate economic opportunities.[45]

I feel we have never, as a country, addressed the Native American issue head-on. It takes leadership and acknowledgment of the sins of the past. Let's help.

So, Elon Musk, if you're reading this!

Robert F. Kennedy, the Compassionate Heart

If I had a time machine, my first action would be to save Bobby Kennedy. Who knows, perhaps Elon Musk will invent one someday. But in all seriousness, Bobby's assassination stole from us the last of our innocence that in 1968 Americans were desperately clinging to. His death put the country into a tailspin that we still have not recovered from. The consequence of Bobby's death was Richard Nixon's presidency, which solidified the existence of political corruption. The return of Camelot 2.0 did not occur, but instead, Tricky Dick's White House of doom and gloom led the country into the political abyss.

Bobby's death sparked the whispers that a Kennedy curse existed, and over time, the family suffered unimaginable losses. Some of these tragedies were self-inflicted, and others were just terrible luck.

An event that struck me as odd occurred when John F. Kennedy, who at the time was a senator from Massachusetts, did an interview with Edward Morrow. "Do you read much?" Morrow asked. JFK responded, "Well, I do have something here that was written by Alan Seeger who, as you'll remember, was born in New York and fought in the Foreign Legion and was killed in the First World War in 1916. He wrote that famous poem, 'I Have a Rendezvous with Death.' Just before he died, he wrote a letter home to his mother which I think has good advice for all of us: 'Whether I am on the winning or the losing side is not the point with me. It is being on the side where my sympathies lie that matters. Success in life means doing that thing then which nothing else conceivable seems more noble or satisfactory or remunerative. And then being ready to see it through to the end.'"[46]

I'm surprised each time I see a photo or a poster of Robert F. Kennedy campaigning in a convertible in Detroit in 1968. As RFK stood on the back of his convertible, people surrounded his car, grabbing his pants leg, touching his shoes, grabbing his arms as if he were the pope. I often wondered what Bobby was thinking. Didn't it ever cross his mind that this is how his brother died—in a convertible? His safety didn't seem to matter to him when he was surrounded by strangers. He shook hundreds of hands on campaign stops and thought nothing of his welfare.

It's painful to think that we lost the Kennedy brothers, cut down in their prime. Neither Kennedy got to see things through to the end. Both Kennedys had a rendezvous with death!

For about ten months after the death of his brother John, Bobby was inconsolable and reported to his job as attorney general each day depressed. In the winter months, he sometimes drove his convertible to work with the roof down, completely unaware; his mind was clearly elsewhere. Robert Kennedy stayed on as attorney general long enough to make sure the 1964 Civil Rights Act was passed, and then he resigned from the Johnson administration.

In the depths of his grief, he received a book from Jackie Kennedy: Edith Hamilton's *The Greek Way*. This book aimed to civilize human beings' primal instincts. Many believed that RFK emerged transformed from this painful period of his life.[47]

The transformation softened Kennedy, who was always seen as his brother's protector. While his toughness remained, another side to Robert Kennedy began to shine—his compassion for the downtrodden. Robert Kennedy transformed his grief into a graceful act for those needing a hero to look up to, someone trustworthy and relatable. Perhaps those who loved him understood he was suffering too, and they needed each other to move forward to live, to carry on his brother's dreams and hopes.

In 1964, Robert F. Kennedy embarked on his own political journey. His determination and ambition led him to win a New York Senate seat on November 3, 1964. This victory was not merely about personal gain; it was about compassion that still to this day touches our American conscience.

In his early career, RFK demonstrated that he was a pit bull, determined and steadfast in his convictions. As a key figure on the rackets committee and later as the attorney general, he had targeted powerful figures like Jimmy Hoffa, the president of the Teamsters Union.

As a newly elected senator from New York, he redirected his fierce sense of justice toward addressing the pressing issues tearing America apart: poverty, racism, and war. The loss of his brother John only furthered his commitment. Now RFK stood as the champion of the underdog, fighting for those who had no voice.[48]

Senator Kennedy's compassion and understanding were on display when he traveled to eastern Kentucky on February 13, 1968. He was a month away from declaring himself a candidate for president and only four months away from his death from an assassin's bullet. He gave no political speeches but moved quietly for two days through the poorest communities in America. His visit to the one-bedroom schoolhouse in Barwick Kentucky made a lasting impression on him and the country. Kennedy asked a little girl, "What did you have to eat today?" William Greider, who worked for the *Louisville Journal*, described Kennedy's "physical humanity." The *Knoxville News Sentinel* said Kennedy, heir to a fortune, "is now one of the faceless hungry."

Indeed, Kennedy struck a chord throughout the country, implying that he was on the side of the downtrodden. His compassion spoke volumes on his two-day visit to Appalachia.[49]

On March 16, 1968, Senator Kennedy declared his candidacy for president. President Johnson announced he would not run for reelection on March 31. On April 2, during a campaign stop in Philadelphia at the Palestra sports arena on the campus of the University of Pennsylvania, Senator Kennedy called for an end to the Vietnam War.

> Everywhere the American people seek not revenge but reconciliation. They seek both at home and abroad solutions of friendship, not force. They seek an end to the war in Vietnam, not through withdrawal or escalation, but through a negotiated settlement in which both sides put away the tools of violence and killing, and labor instead at the conference table for an honorable settlement.

Just two days later, Dr. Martin Luther King, Jr., was struck down by an assassin's bullet as he stood on the balcony of the Ambassador Hotel in Memphis, Tennessee.[50] That same day, Kennedy was campaigning in Indiana at Notre Dame and Ball State University. As he was traveling by plane to Indianapolis, he heard the news of Dr. King's death. Civil rights leader John Lewis helped organize the event. Lewis noted, "There were some people saying that .... Maybe he shouldn't come, because maybe there would be violence. But some of us said he must come."[51]

RFK decided to speak to the crowd when he arrived. Standing on the bed of a pickup truck at 17th and Broadway, an African American neighborhood in Indianapolis, he gave what many consider one of the best impromptu speeches in American history.

> I have bad news for you, for all of our fellow citizens, and people who love peace all over the world, and that is that Martin Luther King was shot and killed tonight.
>
> Martin Luther King dedicated his life to love and to justice for his fellow human beings, and he died because of that effort.
>
> In this difficult day, in this difficult time for the United States, it is perhaps well to ask what kind of a nation we are and what direction we want to move in. For those of you who are black—considering the evidence there evidently is that there were white people who were responsible—you can be filled with bitterness, with hatred, and a desire for revenge. We can move in that direction as a country, in great polarization—black people amongst black, white people amongst white, filled with hatred toward one another.
>
> Or we can make an effort, as Martin Luther King did, to understand and to comprehend, and to replace that violence, that stain of bloodshed that has spread across our land, with an effort to understand with compassion and love.
>
> For those of you who are black and are tempted to be filled with hatred and distrust at the injustice of such an act, against all white people, I can only say that I feel in my own heart the same kind of feeling. I had a member of my family killed, but he was killed by a white man. But we have to make an effort in the United States, we have to make an effort to understand, to go beyond these rather difficult times.

> My favorite poet was Aeschylus. He wrote: "In our sleep, pain which cannot forget falls drop by drop upon the heart until, in our own despair, against our will, comes wisdom through the awful grace of God."
>
> What we need in the United States is not division; what we need in the United States is not hatred; what we need in the United States is not violence or lawlessness; but love and wisdom, and compassion toward one another, and a feeling of justice toward those who still suffer within our country, whether they be white or they be black.
>
> So I shall ask you tonight to return home, to say a prayer for the family of Martin Luther King, that's true, but more importantly to say a prayer for our own country, which all of us love—a prayer for understanding and that compassion of which I spoke.
>
> We can do well in this country. We will have difficult times; we've had difficult times in the past; we will have difficult times in the future. It is not the end of violence; it is not the end of lawlessness; it is not the end of disorder.
>
> But the vast majority of white people and the vast majority of black people in this country want to live together, want to improve the quality of our life, and want justice for all human beings who abide in our land.
>
> Let us dedicate ourselves to what the Greeks wrote so many years ago: to tame the savageness of man and make gentle the life of this world.
>
> Let us dedicate ourselves to that, and say a prayer for our country and for our people.[52]

It took courage for Robert Kennedy to make that speech that night. No one knew how the crowd was going to react. Would they reject his words and riot? Would RFK have to be hustled off by security because of the possibility of violence? Instead, the crowd cheered him. That night, hope looked like a Kennedy!

During those days he spent in Appalachia and on that night in Indianapolis, America caught a glimpse into what kind of president Robert Kennedy might have been. I have no doubt an RFK presidency would have been special. But just sixty-two days later, Robert F. Kennedy met the same fate as Dr. King and his brother John had. On June 5, 1968, celebrating his victory at the California presidential primary, RFK was cut down by an assassin's bullet. Sirhan Sirhan ended the hope of America that night.[53]

Robert Kennedy and Ethel Kennedy were married for eighteen years and had eleven children. A heartbreaking tribute by his son David makes us think of RFK not just as the politician or a grieving brother, but as a father. His son, who was thirteen at the time, wrote his mother a letter as a Christmas gift celebrating his father at the end of a difficult year.

> There will be no more football with Daddy, no more swimming with him, no more riding and no more camping with him. But he was the best father there ever was the best father there ever was and I would rather have him for a father for the length of time I did than any other father for a million years.[54]

It seems death chased Bobby Kennedy down, that it was constantly lurking around every corner he turned. Death of course comes for all of us. We can't deny it, we can't hide from it, we can only try to live our best lives until our time is up. Life is fleeting, but with the time you have left, whether days or years, how will you spend it? Will you be a peacemaker? Will you be compassionate and understanding? Will you spend your time solving problems or creating them? These are questions only you can answer.

Richard M. Nixon, Tricky Dick, and The Chennault Affair

Mark Twain once said, "Truth is stranger than fiction."

This is certainly true when it comes to the Nixon administration's harebrained plot that required a used fire truck, men disguised as firemen, and explosives to blow up the Brookings Institute, a think tank in Washington, D.C.

The intent of this plan was to retrieve files pertaining to the Chennault Affair that were rumored to be in a safe at the think tank. The files could have proven detrimental to President Nixon's re-election if they fell into the wrong hands and were leaked to the public. The plan devised by "plumbers" CIA agent E. Howard Hunt and former FBI agent G. Gordon Liddy was not carried out because, of all things, the cost of the used fire truck!

The following is a transcript of Richard Nixon ordering the only break-in of his presidency.[55]

Date: Thursday, July 1, 1971
Time: 8:45 a.m.–9:52 a.m.
Participants: Richard M. Nixon, H. R. "Bob" Haldeman
Location: Oval Office
Tape: 534-002B
(President Nixon): —get to [John D.] Ehrlichman. Now, will you please get—
(H. R. "Bob" Haldeman): Yeah, we did that.
(President Nixon): I want you to find me a man by noon—I won't be ready till one [o'clock]—till 12:30. A recommendation of the man to work directly with me on this whole situation. You know what I mean? I've got to have—I've got to have one. I mean, I can't have a high-minded lawyer like John Ehrlichman or, you know, [John W.] Dean [III] or somebody like that.

I want a son of a bitch. I want somebody just as tough as I am for a change, just as tough as I *was*, I would say, in the [Alger] Hiss case, where we won the case in the press. These goddamn lawyers, you know, all whining around about, you know...
I'll never forget that they were all so worried about the [Charles] Manson case. I knew exactly what we were doing on the Manson. You got to win some things in the press. These guys don't understand. They have no understanding of politics. They have no understanding of public relations.
John [N.] Mitchell's that way. John [*pounding on the desk*] is always worried about is it technically correct? Do you think, for Christ sakes, the *New York Times* is worried about all the legal niceties? Those sons of bitches are killing them!
They're [*unclear*] by leaking to the press. This is what we've got to get—I want you to shake these [*unclear*] up around here. Now, you do it. Shake them up! Get them off their goddamn dead asses and say, "Now, this is what you should talk about. We're up against an enemy, a conspiracy. They're using any means. [*banging desk for emphasis*] We are going to use any means. Is that clear? [*Haldeman acknowledges.*] Did they get the Brookings Institute raided last night? No?
(Haldeman): No, sir, they didn't.
(President Nixon): Get it done! I want it done! [*banging desk for emphasis*] I want the Brookings Institute safe cleaned out, and have it cleaned out in a way that it makes somebody else [*unclear*].[56]

Nixon was paranoid after the Pentagon Papers were leaked on June 13, 1971, by Daniel Ellsberg, a military analyst. The Pentagon Papers depicted former Presidents Kennedy and Johnson in a dim light regarding truth-telling about the Vietnam war. The Supreme Court ruled 6-3 that President Nixon could not stop the *Washington Post*, *New York Times*, or other news organizations from publishing the Pentagon Papers. Nixon knew that elections could turn on a dime and worried that the next leak could be about him.

Let's revisit the Chennault Affair and the dirty trick Nixon used to win the election of 1968.[57]

On October 31, 1968, President Lyndon B. Johnson publicly announced a halt to the bombing of North Vietnam that could possibly end the Vietnam War. This was a step in the right direction. However, on November 2, South Vietnam walked away from the negotiating table. President Johnson was concerned and upset over these developments.

At the time, the current Democratic Vice President, Hubert Humphrey, was running against the former Republican Vice President Richard Nixon in the presidential race. Governor George Wallace of Alabama was also running in the race as a third party candidate. Nixon and Humphrey were neck and neck. Peace in Vietnam would certainly tip the election to Hubert Humphrey. But Nixon would have none of it, and no dirty trick was off the table even if it meant using American soldiers as political pawns to win the presidency.

Through back channels, Nixon campaign aides communicated with the South Vietnamese to delay the peace talks for a better deal when Richard Nixon became president. Anna Chennault was a Chinese-born Republican fundraiser and widow of Major General Claire Chennault who famously led the World War II Flying Tigers.

President Johnson had the FBI wiretap Anna Chennault as she contacted Vietnam Ambassador Bui Diem and advised him that she had received a message from her boss...which her boss wanted her to give personally to the ambassador. The message was, "hold on. We are going to win....Please tell your boss to hold on."[58]

You have to ask yourself what sort of person would squander peace for political gain. With all the blood that was spilled and lives destroyed, how could anyone knowingly obstruct the chance to end a senseless war? It seems such a person might be devoid of commonsense.

History always has a way of divulging its secrets. With the release of taped phone calls by President Johnson and the Haldeman notes, Nixon's shenanigans regarding the Chennault Affair become quite evident.

After President Johnson's death in 1973, Walt Rostow delivered a package to the LBJ Presidential Library. Rostow served as national security advisor to President Johnson. The package is known as the X envelope or X file. The file was not to be opened for fifty years, but in 1994, the LBJ Library revealed the information pertaining to the Chennault Affair. The library released the telephone conversations in 2008.[59]

President Johnson blamed Nixon for strangling a chance for peace. On November 2, 1968, President Johnson had a telephone conversation with Senator Everette Dirksen. "Johnson says, 'I'm reading their hand, Everett, This is treason.'"[60]

President Johnson had a telephone conversation with Nixon on November 3, 1968, on the matter, but Nixon denied his involvement. "My God," Nixon proclaimed, "I would never do anything to encourage....Saigon not to come to the table. Good God, we want them over in Paris. We've got to get them to Paris or you can't have peace."[61]

In 2017, John A. Farrell uncovered four pages of Haldeman notes while researching his book that were made available to the public after 2007 by the Nixon Library. Bob Haldeman's notes from October 1968 showed that candidate Nixon tried to secretly influence the peace talks while still a presidential candidate and a private citizen.[62]

It is clear that Nixon got away with violating the Logan Act, a federal law (1 Stat. 613;18 U.S.C. §953) aimed at preventing private citizens from conducting foreign affairs without the permission or involvement of the U.S. government. It states:

> Any citizen of the United States, wherever he may be, who, without authority of the United States, directly or indirectly commences or carries on any correspondence or intercourse with any foreign government or any officer or agent thereof, with intent to influence the measures or conduct of any foreign government or of any officer or agent thereof, in relation to any disputes or controversies with the United States, or to defeat the measures of the United States, shall be fined under this title or imprisoned not more than three years, or both.
> This section shall not abridge the right of a citizen to apply, himself or his agent, to any foreign government or the agents thereof for redress of any injury which he may have sustained from such government or any of its agents or subjects.[63]

Many, including President Johnson, thought it was treason. At the time, National Security Advisor Walt Rostow urged President Johnson to "blow the whistle" and destroy Nixon, but President Johnson's hands were tied. However, Exposing this crime would also implicate President

Johnson for his surveillance of an ally and his political opposition. He also did not have solid evidence or Haldeman's notes.[64]

President Nixon remains a polarizing person in history because of his dirty tricks, but he also made some significant contributions to domestic and foreign policies. His journey is a compelling American tale of a Quaker family from California struggling financially and facing personal tragedies. Richard Nixon was born on January 9, 1913, in Yorba Linda, California on his family's lemon farm. Richard had four brothers, two of whom passed away young: Harold tuberculosis at age twenty-three and Arthur at age seven of tuberculosis encephalitis.

Nixon's mother came to believe her son had survivor's guilt. "Unconsciously I think Richard may have felt a kind of guilt…he was alive," Hannah concluded. "It seems that Richard was trying to be three sons in one, striving even harder than before to make up for our loss."[65]

The lemon farm eventually failed, forcing the family to move to Whittier, California in 1922. The Nixon grocery store emerged, requiring young Richard to rise at 3 a.m. and drive to Los Angeles to buy vegetables at the farmers market. The family suffered through the Great Depression and severe dust storms but pushed forward.[66]

Richard learned the importance of hard work and discipline. Poor but proud, Richard's father was very tough on him, verbally abusive at times, and his mother was the epitome of a religious Quaker woman who always made sure Richard went to school wearing a crisp white shirt.[67]

Richard found an escape in reading. His parents bought him books about American heroes. Richard's grandmother gave him verses by Longfellow for inspiration that hung over his bed.[68]

Nixon's plan for attending an Ivy league school was derailed because he was needed at home to help with the family business. Instead, he attended Whittier College and was involved in student government drama and sports. Nixon played football, but only because the team needed participants, not because he was an exceptional athlete. Nixon's mind, not sports, was his most powerful tool. In 1937, he graduated from Whittier College with a degree in history and received a scholarship to Duke University School of Law, where he graduated third in his class.[69]

Richard Nixon served in World War II, when he learned the art of poker and racked up roughly $10,000. Winning at poker requires knowing your opponent and taking calculated risks. Nixon quickly moved up the political ladder as congressman, senator, and then the youngest vice president ever at thirty-nine in the Eisenhower administration.

Nixon was viewed as an anti-communist crusader. He waged a campaign of dirty tricks against his political opponents. He defeated Jerry Voorhis in the 1946 race for the House of Representatives, which represented California's Twelfth District. As a congressman, Nixon was involved in the Alger Hiss case. Hiss was a former government official accused of being a Soviet spy. Nixon held a committee position on the Un-American Activities Committee (HUAC) and went after Hiss like a dog after a bone.

Hiss did jail time, and Nixon's status was elevated nationally. He ran for senator of California against Helen Gahagan Douglas. He won and served as senator of California from 1950–1953, earning the nickname "Tricky Dick" for again running a dirty campaign against his opponent.

These political victories appealed to Dwight D. Eisenhower, who made Nixon his vice president for two terms. However, the vice presidency almost didn't happen for Nixon because he was faced with his first major political controversy involving campaign donations. Nixon had to plead his case on national television that he was not using campaign funds to live a lavish lifestyle. This speech is famously known as the "Checkers speech" and it showed Nixon's uncanny political ability to draw on public sympathies.

Nixon's only crime that he would admit to was receiving a gift of an American cocker spaniel that his children loved and named "Checkers." The speech made Eisenhower comfortable with having Nixon on the ticket.[70]

His political career took a nosedive when he suffered back-to-back defeats. The first major loss was against John F. Kennedy in the race for president in 1960. Many believed, including Nixon, that the race was stolen in Texas and Chicago, but no protest was filed.

Many thought Nixon's second loss would be the last time we saw him on the political stage. His failed quest for the governorship of California in 1962 cut him like a knife. Democrat Pat Brown was victorious, and Nixon gave one of his most memorable press conferences. A defiant and defeated

Nixon proclaimed, "You don't have Nixon to kick around anymore, because gentlemen, this is my last press conference."[71]

Professor Luke A. Nichter, who is a coauthor of *The Nixon Tapes 1971–1972* with Douglass Brinkley, said something many agree with: "Nixon really is like a prism, you know, you can turn it any way you want, and the light will hit it in different ways."[72]

It seems that one aspect of Nixon's persona was a darkness he could never escape. The other aspect was grit, a determination to make a difference, and a long laundry list of presidential accomplishments.

Nixon abolished the draft and transitioned the U.S. military to an all-volunteer force. To the surprise of many a Republican, Nixon established the Environmental Protection Agency. He waged war on cancer and allocated $100 million for the cause. He promoted gender equality and signed Title IX. He oversaw the desegregation of Southern schools and also supported the Twenty-sixth Amendment to lower the voting age from twenty-one to eighteen. He granted Native Americans tribal self-determination and returned sacred lands to them.

Nixon made a positive mark on foreign policy. His diplomatic efforts with the Soviet Union were noble, aiming to reduce Cold War tensions through Strategic Arms Limitation Talks (SALT). Nixon also signed the Anti-ballistic Missile (ABM) treaty with the Soviets. Nixon famously visited China in 1972, opening up relations and cooling tensions between the two countries. Nixon ended the Vietnam War through the Paris Peace Accords in 1973.[73]

President Nixon most certainly thought about how history would remember him. JFK, the man who beat him in 1960, was immortalized in a striking White House portrait. With his head down and arms folded, Kennedy is depicted as a thinking president, an inspirational leader. What will they write about Nixon? Would the historians just focus on Watergate and nothing else?

Nixon will always be in a perpetual state of rehabilitation. He strove to change the narrative about himself from a disgraced political leader to an expert in foreign policy. After he resigned the presidency, he consulted with presidents on America's role in the world, wrote eleven books, and traveled abroad in a desperate attempt to rewrite his legacy.

Unfortunately, despite his efforts, Nixon will always be viewed like a car wreck that you can't take your eyes off when you drive past it. Ted Koppel hosted a popular show called *Nightline* from 1980 to 2005. Koppel began an interview of the former president on January 7, 1992, with the statement: "Anytime you appear since 1974, there is always a chorus of criticisms, saying why are you putting that man on television, he disgraced the office of the presidency. Shouldn't be there, you shouldn't be listening to what he has to say."[74]

I found it ironic and interesting that in Richard Nixon's book *Leaders*, he writes, "People may like the boy next door, but that does not mean they want him as their president, or even as a congressman. The successful leader does not talk down to people. He lifts them up. He must never be arrogant."[75] Perhaps we see Nixon's reflective side here, wishing for a do-over in his role as commander in chief.

Even in death some people perceive Richard Nixon as a crook, almost subhuman, evoking a strong visceral reaction. When Nixon died, colorful journalist Hunter S. Thompson, a "gonzo journalist," wrote an unforgettable obituary. Here is an excerpt:

DATE: MAY 1, 1994
FROM: DR. HUNTER S. THOMPSON
SUBJECT: THE DEATH OF RICHARD NIXON: NOTES ON THE PASSING OF AN AMERICAN MONSTER.... HE WAS A LIAR AND A QUITTER, AND HE SHOULD HAVE BEEN BURIED AT SEA.... BUT HE WAS, AFTER ALL, THE PRESIDENT.
I have had my own bloody relationship with Nixon for many years, but I am not worried about it landing me in hell with him. I have already been there with that bastard, and I am a better person for it. Nixon had the unique ability to make his enemies seem honorable, and we developed a keen sense of fraternity. Some of my best friends have hated Nixon all their lives. My mother hates Nixon, my son hates Nixon, I hate Nixon, and this hatred has brought us together.

Nixon laughed when I told him this. "Don't worry," he said, "I, too, am a family man, and we feel the same way about you."

It was Richard Nixon who got me into politics, and now that he's gone, I feel lonely. He was a giant in his way. As long as Nixon was politically alive—and he was, all the way to the end—we could always be sure of finding the enemy on the Low Road. There was no need to look anywhere else for the evil bastard. He had the fighting instincts of a badger trapped by hounds. The badger will roll over on its back and emit a smell of death, which confuses the dogs and lures them in for the traditional ripping and tearing action. But it is usually the badger who does the ripping and tearing. It is a beast that fights best on its back: rolling under the throat of the enemy and seizing it by the head with all four claws.

That was Nixon's style—and if you forgot, he would kill you as a lesson to the others. Badgers don't fight fair, bubba. That's why God made dachshunds.

If the right people had been in charge of Nixon's funeral, his casket would have been launched into one of those open-sewage canals that empty into the ocean just south of Los Angeles. He was a swine of a man and a jabbering dupe of a president. Nixon was so crooked that he needed servants to help him screw his pants on every morning. Even his funeral was illegal. He was queer in the deepest way. His body should have been burned in a trash bin.[76]

Even though what Thompson writes is political satire, therein lies some truth about the man, President Nixon who spent a career fighting in the political gutter.

As for escaping the darkness, some believe Nixon's successes will always be second fiddle to his criminal activity, which forced him to resign the presidency of the United States.

George Floyd, We Shall Overcome

Did violence and property destruction overshadow George Floyd's murder? How can we reconnect with Dr. King's vision of nonviolence?

Reflecting on George Floyd's murder at forty-six years of age still makes me think we have much work to do with race relations in this country. His murder on May 25, 2020, has left many angry and frustrated to this day. Police were called to a convenience store in Minneapolis where George Floyd allegedly attempted to buy cigarettes with a counterfeit $20 bill. The murder was caught on video as Minneapolis police officer Derek Chauvin pressed his knee onto Floyd's neck for nine minutes and twenty-nine seconds. In the trial of officer Chauvin, the judge sentenced him to twenty-two and a half years in prison.[77]

While his murder sparked a nationwide conversation about police brutality and systemic racism, the destruction of city businesses is not an appropriate response to this tragedy. It's understandable that people were angry and frustrated, but it's more important to channel that energy into constructive action that can bring about real change. This might include supporting local businesses, volunteering with community organizations, or advocating for policy changes that address the root causes of systemic racism.

The violence after George Floyd's murder didn't solve the problem, but instead spread hardship through property destruction. The damage was quite extensive, with estimated costs ranging from $1 to $2 billion. Minneapolis was center stage in this protest, but other cities saw major unrest, including New York, Los Angeles, Washington, D.C., and Atlanta. Peaceful protests also occurred throughout other parts of the country. I remember the news bringing us live coverage of some cities on fire and the looting that took place. Violence and race riots have always been an unfortunate part of American history, rattling our nerves and making us ask whether we can all just get along. Change is possible, but it requires sustained effort and a commitment to nonviolent action. By working together and supporting one another, we can create a more just and equitable society.[78]

 We should never forget the effectiveness of Dr. Martin Luther King's nonviolent resistance. King, a Baptist preacher by trade, had a passion for Christ and love of his fellow man. King said, "The time is always right to do what is right." What King did right was changing the hearts and minds of the entire country. Citizens all over turned to their televisions and newspapers, witnessing King and his followers protesting nonviolently as they were sprayed with high-power hoses, beaten by police officers, and arrested for practicing their First Amendment rights. Americans began asking, "What kind of country is this?"

 King's great influence was Christ, but Henry David Thoreau's book *Civil Disobedience* also piqued his interest in the idea of resisting unjust laws peacefully. As a result, King was arrested twenty-nine times on phony charges as he protested in a nonviolent fashion. King was also motivated by Mahatma Gandhi, who practiced nonviolent resistance and helped India gain independence. He ended up paying ultimate price for his leadership when he was assassinated.[79]

We know that as Dr. King protested, he received threats on his life constantly. He met his demise by an assassin's bullet, but not before making a significant impact on America. The Civil Rights Movement continues to this day because it carried a positive message that echoed with love, not hate. [80]

I'm thankful justice was served in the George Floyd case, but I'm afraid that his murder, which should have been front and center in the eyes of the world, got diminished in the aftermath of violence and destruction. As Dr. King said, "Hate begets hate; violence begets violence; toughness begets a greater toughness. We must meet the forces of hate with the power of love."[81]

Ronald Reagan, in Love with America

Back in the 1990s, my grandmother lived in public housing and had some interesting neighbors—some kind and thoughtful, others not much so. There was a man down the hallway that would knock on my grandmother's door and ask for a sandwich, and she would always make it for him or give him a glass of milk, cheese, eggs, or whatever he needed. I always told my grandmother her apartment wasn't a local grocery store, but she smiled and said she was glad to help. She was definitely a lovely person who didn't have much for herself, especially after my grandfather died.

Another neighbor, Louise, often needed help, and my grandmother would ask me to assist her with moving things such as furniture or bringing in the groceries. What always caught my eye was a painting of Ronald Reagan hanging in her living room.

Before his political career, Reagan was a Hollywood actor who appeared in over fifty movies, starting in the late 1930s with films like *Knute Rockne, All American* and *Bedtime for Bonzo*. He even served as the president of the Screen Actors Guild. He later served as the thirty-third governor of California from 1967 to 1975.[82]

Both my grandmother and Louise adored Reagan and were no fans of Bill Clinton in the 1990s. They spoke for hours about how Clinton disgraced the office with Monica Lewinsky, something they believed Reagan would never do. I agreed.

President Reagan was a romantic who loved his country and his wife. He often left little notes around the White House for Nancy, and he had a jar of jelly beans on his desk, preferring the blueberry-flavored ones. He loved spending time at his California ranch and was often seen wearing a cowboy hat and riding on his horse. Louise once told me, "Reagan was the last cowboy, and I thought he was the greatest President ever." I didn't argue with her, although I could have made a strong case for Lincoln.

I understood their connection to Reagan—to them, he felt like a good neighbor. They shared a lot in common, having gone through a Great Depression and World War II, sacrificed, suffered, and ultimately been victorious together.

The historians, however, have different ideas of who they think was the greatest president of all time.

Let's take a look at what many consider the gold standard of presidential rankings: C-Span. Do I feel that Ronald Reagan's ranking is accurate here? I do not. I believe Reagan should be ranked above Kennedy, and I would feel comfortable with Reagan at 5 instead of 9. While I admire President Kennedy, I don't think he served long enough to be ranked in the top 10, although his inspiration definitely impacted his placement. I would rate Reagan above Eisenhower.

1. Abraham Lincoln
2. George Washington
3. Franklin D. Roosevelt
4. Theodore Roosevelt

5. Dwight D. Eisenhower

6. Harry S. Truman

7. Thomas Jefferson

8. John F. Kennedy

9. Ronald Reagan

10. Barack Obama[83]

When you consider President Reagan's accomplishments, I don't think Louise was that far off from her number one ranking of Reagan.

Reagan's Accomplishments

Cut taxes through the Economic Recovery Tax Act of August 13, 1981, and sought to deregulate the economy

Appointed the first woman to the Supreme Court, Sandra Day O'Connor, on July 7, 1981

Signed Social Security reform for long-term solvency on April 20, 1983

Increased defense spending and built up the United States military for "Peace through Strength"

Launched the Strategic Defense Initiative on March 23, 1983, which led to the development of the Patriot Defense System. This idea continues to evolve as new technologies are developed.

Launched the War on Drugs—Nancy Reagan's "Just Say No Campaign"—on September 14, 1986

Signed the Immigration Reform and Control Act on November 6, 1986, which granted amnesty to millions of undocumented immigrants

Gave the famous "Mr. Gorbachev, tear down this wall" speech on June 12, 1987. The Berlin Wall came down during George H. W. Bush's presidency.

Signed the Intermediate-Range Nuclear Forces Treaty on December 8, 1987, with Soviet leader Mikhail Gorbachev.

Played a significant role in ending the Cold War by building up the military and through his diplomatic efforts.[84]

If I could, I would add optimism to this list. Optimism and a strong sense of morality were Reagan's key traits. His positivity opened many doors, each one more significant than the last. Reagan's belief in right and wrong and good and evil helped steer the country back on course.

Reagan's goals were clear in his Republican National Convention speech in Kansas City, Missouri, on August 19, 1976. His message resonated and eventually propelled him into the Oval Office in 1980.

> There are cynics who say that a party platform is something that no one bothers to read and it doesn't very often amount to much. Whether it is different this time than it has ever been before, I believe the Republican party has a platform that is a banner of bold, unmistakable colors with no pale pastel shades.[85]

Where did Ronald Reagan's optimism come from? He was born to John and Nellie Reagan in Tampico, Illinois, on February 6, 1911. Despite suffering from the Irish flu, John still had a significant impact on his son's life. As a shoe salesmen, he felt discriminated against by signs that read "No Dogs or Irish Need Apply" and always stood for tolerance. His parents did not share the same religion. Reagan's mother was a Protestant, and his father was Catholic.

His father was adamant that no one should be discriminated against because of religion and felt the same regarding skin color. Ronald Reagan once stated, "The biggest sin in his eyes was racial or religious preference." His father believed in this so strongly that he once slept in his car on a business trip in a blizzard because the hotel clerk said no Jews were allowed. His mother seemed to have made the greatest impact on him and his brother. Reagan commented, "My brother and I, we were truly influenced by our mother, who was truly religious but also a great kindness she had. We were a rather poor family, and yet my mother was always finding people worse off than we were that she could bring help to." His mother believed that everyone was a child of God.

Ronald Reagan learned these life lessons well. When Reagan attended Eureka College, he played on the football team. The team had an away game, and the hotel owner told the coach the black football players could not stay there. Reagan took charge and informed his coach that the two black players could come home with him because his house was nearby. Reagan knew his parents would welcome them and they did, with open arms.[86]

President Reagan was only in office for just about nine weeks when on March 30, 1981, after wrapping up a speech with the Construction Trade Council, a union group at the Hilton, just a mile from the White House, he was shot. The assassin was twenty-five-year-old John Hinckley, Jr., who later confessed to wanting to be like the character Travis Bickle in *Taxi Driver*. Hinckley wanted to impress the actress Jodie Foster by shooting the president.

Shots were fired, first striking James Brady squarely in the head and a Washington Metro officer Thomas K. Delahanty in the spine. Another shot struck Secret Service Agent Tim McCarthy in the torso. The shot that hit Reagan ricocheted off the presidential car. Secret Service agent Jerry Parr shoved Reagan into the presidential limo and the two tried to figure out if he had been hit. As they left the scene, three men lay on the sidewalk, their lives hanging in the balance.

Reagan walked into the emergency room under his own power, but once he entered, he collapsed. What many Americans don't realize is how close the seventy-year-old was to death. The bullet had entered through his armpit and gone through his lung.

In a sort of life imitating art moment that Reagan portrayed when he played Lieutenant "Brass" Bancroft in the 1939 film *Code of the Secret Service*, now he needed the protection as a president.

Reagan's grace under fire, his optimism while he lay in his hospital bed, are the stories that Americans gravitate to and remember.

Reagan used humor in his time of distress, telling his wife, "Honey, I forgot to duck." When told that he would have to be operated on, Reagan quipped, "I just hope you're all Republicans." A doctor replied, "Today, Mr. President, we're all Republicans."[87]

Of course, like most presidents, Reagan had his share of controversies. For one, he would by no means wear a cardigan sweater in the White House like his predecessor did. This angered many who wanted to wean the country off fossil fuels. Carter tried to rally Americans to save energy by trying to convince them to turn their thermostats down. Reagan, on the other hand, removed the solar panels from the White House roof and turned up the heat. He wanted to reduce the dependency on foreign oil and increase domestic production, believing this was important to America's national security and that it was a sign of strength.[88]

Reagan found himself in another controversy when he addressed the air traffic controllers strike in August 1981. The air traffic controllers wanted better working conditions and higher wages. President Reagan gave the strikers forty-eight hours to reach an agreement. When time was up, he fired 11,359 striking workers. His action haunted the Republican party for some time. Democrats ran ads against their Republican opponents claiming that they were anti-worker.[89]

The biggest threat to Ronald Reagan's presidency became public in November 1986. The incident involved a secret U. S arms deal that traded weapons to Iran for the release of American hostages in Lebanon. The funds gained from this deal were illegal under U.S. law and were used to support Contra rebels in Nicaragua. Reagan denied his involvement.

Lieutenant Colonel Oliver North of the National Security Council admitted he was responsible and had diverted funds to the Contras. North, Reagan's National Security Advisor Robert McFarland from 1983–1985, and John Poindexter, Reagan's National security advisor from 1985–1986, were all found guilty, but their convictions were overturned or their sentences were minimal. However, the scandal damaged President Reagan's credibility with the American people.

Reagan addressed the nation from the Oval Office, stating, "A few months ago I told the American people I did not trade arms for hostages. My heart and best intentions still tell me that's true, but the facts and evidence tell me it's not." He admitted fault, and the country forgave him, although some in the media tried to compare Iran-Contra to Watergate. The comparison never amounted to much, and Reagan continued to press forward. Some questioned his age and memory, but President Reagan went on to restore the confidence that the American people placed in him.[90]

Ronald Reagan was the guy you would want to have a beer with because he had a great wit and humor. He was called the "Great Communicator" for a reason. Like President Franklin Roosevelt, who used his calming voice to reassure his people during his "Fireside Chats" on the radio during the Great Depression, President Reagan understood that to be an effective president, you have to be relatable and talk about the issues that people care about. Reagan's acting experience certainly played a role in his ability to connect with people, both on radio and TV as president.

I often think Ronald Reagan would have made a fantastic history teacher. He was a great storyteller, and whoever tells the best story keeps the students' attention. In this case, the students are aware of the American citizens from the sticks of Tennessee to streets of New York City. Reagan gave history lessons on his radio addresses that tugged at heartstrings and infused the American spirit into the listener. His speeches and talks on the radio often hit the mark and captured America's greatness

For example, Reagan discussed George Washington and the pain and suffering that occurred at Valley Forge. He said, "George Washington knelt in prayer at Valley Forge and in the darkest days of our struggle for independence said that 'the fate of unborn millions will now depend, under God, on the courage and conduct of this army.'" It was apparent that Reagan thought if God was on your side, you can't lose.[91]

In another radio address, Reagan reminded Americans of our history and how we fought to keep it.

> Such is the story behind our Star-Spangled Banner. It was two years into the War of 1812, and America seemed to be teetering on the edge of defeat. The British had already taken our capital and burned the White House. Baltimore was the next target in a grand design to divide our forces and crush this newly independent nation of upstart colonies. All that stood between the British and Baltimore were the guns of Fort McHenry, blocking their entry into Baltimore Harbor. The British bombardment lasted 25 hours. Through the dark hours of the night, the rockets fired and the bombs exploded. And a young American named Key, held captive aboard a ship, watched anxiously for some proof, some sign, that liberty would prevail. You can imagine his joy when the next morning, in the dawn's light, he looked out and saw the banner flying-a little tattered and torn, but still flying proudly above the ramparts.[92]

Another example of Reagan's ability to connect was when he referred to the boys of Pointe du Hoc in a speech on the fortieth anniversary of D-

Day, or in 1986, when the world watched the space shuttle *Challenger* explode and America wept over the tragic loss of the seven astronauts. President Reagan quoted John Gillespie Magee's poem "High Flight," saying they had "slipped the surly bonds of earth to touch the face of God." The words made us appreciate their courage and sacrifice for space exploration. As American students and teachers mourned the loss of Christa McAuliffe, who was going to be the first teacher in space, President Reagan's words brought comfort and inspiration.

President Reagan understood moments in history and how his position as leader of the free world could bring about change, not just in America, but around the world. His speech at the Brandenburg Gate Berlin on June 12, 1987, emphasized his strength and vision.

> Behind me stands a wall that encircles the free sectors of this city, part of a vast system of barriers that divides the entire continent of Europe.... Standing before the Brandenburg Gate, every man is a German, separated from his fellow men. Every man is a Berliner, forced to look upon a scar.... As long as this gate is closed, as long as this scar of a wall is permitted to stand, it is not the German question alone that remains open, but the question of freedom for all mankind....
> General Secretary Gorbachev, if you seek peace, if you seek prosperity for the Soviet Union and Eastern Europe, if you seek liberalization, come here to this gate.
> Mr. Gorbachev, open this gate!
> Mr. Gorbachev, tear down this wall![93]

Ronald Reagan was not afraid to tell it like it is. He once called the Soviet Union "The Evil Empire." President Reagan understood who our friends and enemies in the world were. The fortieth president often used the phrase "trust but verify" when he was discussing arms control and nuclear disarmament with the Soviets. The phrase became internationally known in English after Suzanne Massie, a scholar of Russian history, taught it to Ronald Reagan, who used it in discussions of nuclear disarmament with the Soviet Union.[94]

President Reagan's style and grace were unmatched, as when he met with Soviet leader Gorbachev in Iceland. He won over the Soviet leader, and the two struck up a friendship that helped end the Cold War. He had an ability to simplify complex issues, as demonstrated by his foreign policy of "peace through strength." This powerful message sent a clear signal to our adversaries that the United States will fight for and defend itself at all costs.

As the world's leading superpower, we have a responsibility to use our strength to make the world a safer place. We should encourage our allies to do what is necessary to achieve this goal. The United States should lead by example, leveraging our military and economic power to ensure global security. We must never forget that our place in the world is at the top, and we should never surrender our position of strength.

Even in his post-presidency, Reagan showed optimism in the face of his Alzheimer's diagnosis. He remained hopeful about the "Shining City on the Hill" and the American people. An excerpt from his letter announcing his illness struck me, revealing that Reagan's message remained consistent throughout his life. On November 5, 1994, five years after leaving office, Reagan penned this heartfelt letter.

Unfortunately, as Alzheimer's Disease progresses, the family often bears a heavy burden. I only wish there was some way I could spare Nancy from this painful experience. When the time comes I am confident that with your help she will face faith and courage.

In closing let me thank you, the American people, for giving me the great honor of allowing me to serve as your President. When the Lord calls me home, whenever that may be, I will leave with the greatest love for this country of ours and eternal optimism for its future.

I now begin the journey that will lead me into the sunset of my life. I know that for America there will always be a bright dawn ahead....

Is the Reagan presidency a lesson in optimism? Can we shed this cynicism and political polarization that plagues America? The idea of a civil war today over who wins the presidency seems odd to me. What would that look like? Blue states versus red states? What about your neighbors on your street who think differently than you? Are we really going to have a call to arms like we did in 1861? This is not a sectional issue in which one part of the country can leave the union over who wins the presidency. Unfortunately, I do think violence will become more prevalent in major cities as a result of future presidential elections. In Reagan's inaugural address in January 1981, he firmly highlighted the importance of an orderly transfer of power. He thanked his predecessor, President Carter, for his cooperation during the transition process.[95]

Despite Reagan's optimism, historically, our democracy has been messy. Half the country doesn't believe in your politics and most likely can't tolerate your presidential candidate. When did this bad blood in politics start? Some would say the election of 1800, President John Adams versus his Vice President, Thomas Jefferson. The one constant since the election of 1800 is that politics have been fought in the sewer, and by the end of the process, no one comes out clean. You might ask yourself who in their right mind would want to run for president and put themselves through this process. The oppositional research teams will do their homework, interviewing friends and enemies and past employees, looking for dirt that can end up on the front page of *The Washington Post* because, after all, democracy dies in the darkness.

You always have to give credit where it is due. President Washington hit the head on the nail when, during his farewell address on September 17, 1796, he said, "However political parties may now and then answer popular ends, they are likely in the course of time and things, to become potent engines, by which cunning, ambitious, and unprincipled men will be enabled to subvert the power of the people and to usurp for themselves the reins of government, destroying afterwards the very engines which have lifted them to unjust dominion."[96]

It is wise to remember Washington's words. Even though it seems we're stuck with political parties, we must prioritize being American citizens over our political affiliations. In America, we should be grateful for the freedom to express our political beliefs without fear of persecution or legal consequences. Our commitment to the First Amendment sustains us during uncertain times—times when we must raise our voices, even if they diverge from those of our neighbors or our government. Our constitution distinguishes us from the rest of the world and serves as a bedrock for people of all backgrounds: gay, straight, Black, Latino, White, religious, atheist, Republican, Democrat, Independent—everyone can thrive here, everyone can be heard. Indeed, the Constitution acts as kryptonite against the deep-seated hatred some harbor toward Americans with different opinions.

I read an article in *Vanity Fair* by Christopher Hitchens, a liberal writer and thinker, titled "Visit to a Small Planet" in January 2001. The article stayed with me as a reminder of how fortunate I am to be an American. Hitchens wrote about destitute and inescapable North Korea, where the only way to leave was to die. The article always made me think, how lucky are we? Yes, life is not perfect in America, but we can still achieve our dreams, grow in our faith, and be who we want to be.

In modern times, cable news, YouTube, and social media devote hours to ridiculing presidents or candidates for higher office, often mocking them or censoring information before an election, such as the case of Hunter Biden's laptop. Some suggest these search and destroy missions started with Nixon, leading to his resignation on August 9, 1974. Regardless, Nixon was caught red-handed and was fortunate to get a pardon from President Ford.

In recent years, you hear some strange political stories that make you scratch your head in disbelief, like claims that President Obama was Muslim, not a Christian, or was born outside the country, and therefore should have never been president. My favorite is that President Donald Trump was a Russian agent working for the Kremlin. I always laughed at both Obama and Trump stories because they were so ridiculous and were egged on by the press. Depending on what channel you watch or which newspapers you read, you can find information that fits your narrative and what you believe. I'm not a partisan here, I'm just calling balls and strikes as I see them.

With all the corrosive cynicism, there remains the continued threat that some crackpot will assassinate our president. So yes, there are serious flaws in our system and at the same time a danger for those serving as president or seeking the highest office in the land.

In President Reagan's inaugural address as governor of California in 1967, he understood a fundamental principle that America and freedom were precious and should not be taken for granted. I personally feel it is important to celebrate our different political voices instead of vilifying each other.

> Freedom is never more than one generation from extinction. We didn't pass it to our children in the bloodstream. It must be fought for, protected and handed on for them to do the same, or one day we will spend our sunset years telling our children and our children's children what it was once like in the United States when men were free.[97]

John Winthrop, the governor of the Massachusetts Bay Colony, first used the phrase "a city on a hill" in a sermon he delivered in 1630. However, it was President Ronald Reagan who brought that phrase to life in his farewell address to the nation from the Oval Office on January 11, 1989. President Reagan gave a number of memorable speeches during his time in the White House, but his farewell speech struck me as the expression of a man who truly understood what America was all about.

In his speech, President Reagan spoke of the shining city on a hill, a phrase that he had used throughout his political career. He described it as a tall, proud city built on rocks stronger than oceans, windswept, God-blessed, and teeming with people of all kinds living in harmony and peace. It was a city with free ports that hummed with commerce and creativity, and if there had to be city walls, their doors were open to anyone with the will and the heart to get here.[98]

President Reagan's vision of America as a shining city on a hill was powerful, and it still resonates. He saw America as a beacon of freedom and hope, a magnet for all who seek a better life. Even after two centuries, America still stands strong and true on the granite ridge, her glow holding steady no matter what storm is raging.

Looking back, I have fond memories of Louise and my grandmother sitting around the table in public housing, having a coffee, talking about the good old days and President Reagan. They were not wealthy, but like Reagan, they were always rich with optimism.

Admiral James Stockdale, A Stoic Mind

> It's not what happens to you, but how you react to it that matters.—Epictetus[99]

Throughout history, people have pondered the questions "Who am I?" and "Why am I here?" However, these profound questions had never been posed on a national debate stage until Admiral Stockdale did so during the vice presidential debate in 1992. If social media had existed then, his question would have undoubtedly gone viral and broken the internet. This statement was too deep for a political debate, leaving people scratching their heads, unable to grasp the depth of this American hero. Pundits and comedians seized on Stockdale's words, turning him into a punchline overnight.

The 1992 vice presidential debate between Senator Al Gore, Vice President Dan Quayle, and Admiral James Bond Stockdale was certainly memorable. Stockdale survived being a prisoner of war, but he did not survive the political fallout of the debate. Bill Clinton's campaign manager, James Carville went on to famously say, "It's the economy, stupid," and he was right. The younger duo of Clinton and Gore, whose energetic theme song was "Don't Stop Thinking about Tomorrow," went on to defeat the incumbent George H. W. Bush, the feisty businessman Ross Perot, and the misunderstood Admiral Stockdale.

Stockdale said his experience as a vice presidential candidate, "There are certain things I'm good at. Fighter pilot I'm good at. I was damn good at leading a prison underground. But vice president? That was a lark."[100]

James Bond Stockdale was born a Protestant in Abingdon, Illinois, in 1923. He earned a college degree from the United States Naval Academy and graduated in 1946. Stockdale studied philosophy at Stanford University while earning a master's degree in international relations in 1962. Stockdale was inspired by the philosopher Epictetus, who was born a slave in about A.D. 50. Epictetus' master Epaphroditus brought him to Rome, where he later studied with Musonius Rufus. When Emperor Domitian banished the philosophers from Rome, Epictetus established a school of philosophy on the northwest coast of Greece in Nicopolis.

Epictetus centered his teaching on several principles: mastering your desires; performing your duties; and thinking clearly about yourself and your relationships with others.[101]

Stockdale's plane, an A-4 Skyhawk, was shot down after he took off from the USS *Oriskany* over northern Vietnam. Stoicism helped him endure captivity in the Hoa Lo Prison, often referred to as the "Hanoi Hilton," from September 9, 1965, until February 12, 1973.

> After ejection I had about thirty seconds to make my last statement in freedom before I landed in the main street of a little village right ahead. And so help me, I whispered to myself: "Five years down there, at least. I'm leaving the world of technology and entering the world of Epictetus."[102]

The treatment Admiral Stockdale endured was horrifying. He spent over seven years as a prisoner of war and four years in leg irons in solitary confinement. He inflicted harm on himself to avoid being used as propaganda, and once he slit his scalp with a razor. In one desperate moment, he slit his wrist to kill himself to prevent the enemy from extracting information. Stockdale was subjected to whippings, beatings that nearly took his life, and near-asphyxiation with ropes. He was denied medical care and deprived of letters from home. His fellow prisoners held him in high regard because he developed methods to resist enemy propaganda.[103]

Stockdale used Epictetus' teachings as a secret weapon during captivity. Stockade wrote in his book *Courage on Fire*, "What Epictetus was telling his students was there can be no such thing as being the 'victim' of another. You can only be a 'victim' of yourself. It's all in how you discipline your mind. Who is your master? "He who has authority over any of the things on which you have set your heart." What is the result at which all virtue aims? Serenity." Show me a man who, though sick is happy, who though in danger is happy, who though in prison is happy, and I'll show you a Stoic."[104]

James Stockdale was finally released on February 12, 1973. He sadly proclaimed, "I was tortured fifteen times, that's total submission. They did that by shutting off your blood circulation with ropes, giving you claustrophobia and pain at the same time, bending you double."[105] Stockdale's wife and four sons suffered immensely. not knowing if he was dead or alive. His wife Sybil, however, did not sit idly by, but advocated for the rights of Vietnam prisoners of war.[106]

President Gerald Ford presented James Bond Stockdale with the Medal of Honor in 1976 and praised his heroic resistance and indomitable spirit. President Reagan later described Stockdale as one of the bravest men he ever met. Later on, James Stockdale was president of the Naval War College from 1977–1979 and then president of the Citadel from 1979–1980.

Along with the Medal of Honor, Admiral Stockdale received the following:

Distinguished Service Medal with two stars

Silver Star with three stars

Legion of Merit with Combat "V"

Distinguished Flying Cross with one star

Bronze Star w/Combat "V" and one star

Purple Heart with one star

Air Medal

Combat Action Ribbon

Unit Commendation

Prisoner of War Medal

American Campaign Medal

World War II Victory Medal

Occupation Service Medal

National Defense Service Medal with one star

Armed Forces Expeditionary Medal

Sea Service Deployment Ribbon with six stars

Vietnam Service Medal

Vietnam Campaign Medal[107]

Admiral Stockdale's portrait should have hung in every president's oval office since he was released as a POW for several reasons. First, he was an American hero, and America will forever be indebted to him for his courage and sacrifice. Second, his capture and torture should make our government ask if we are making wise decisions regarding war.

The military tribute at Vice Admiral Stockdale's funeral on July 5, 2005, was well deserved. When we see the flags on the coffins of heroes, I immediately think of the meaning and significance of our flag. The red stands for valor and bravery, the white represents purity and innocence, and the blue signifies vigilance, perseverance, and justice. The stripes symbolize the original thirteen colonies that declared their independence from Great Britain.

As citizens, we view our American flags in different settings across the country. We see our flag flying on barns, on boats, on military ships, on the backs of pickup trucks, on houses throughout the homeland. When I view our flag, I think of Admiral Stockdale in solitary confinement in the darkness, but never surrendering. We should also never forget the more than one-half million Americans who have been captured and interned as POWs since the American Revolution.[108]

Vietnam was widely known as a tragic mistake aimed at stopping the spread of Communism—a goal that proved unrealistic. The American soldier fought courageously in the jungles of Vietnam, in the air, and on the sea, in a country that they were unfamiliar with, against an enemy that was well-versed in the terrain. The Vietcong's stealthy guerrilla tactics led to the deaths of 58,220 U.S. soldiers. This was the consequence of waging an ill-advised war, a war that divided our country with protests that in many cases targeted the American soldiers, who were sacrificed because their leaders sent them to battle.[109]

Vietnam should have served as a reminder about how not to conduct foreign policy. Before sending our soldiers to war, we need to ask numerous questions: What is your goal of your mission? What is the entrance strategy? What is your exit strategy? The fall of Saigon, which involved evacuating thousands of South Vietnamese and Americans, signaled to the world America's failure there.

Since the end of the Vietnam war, we have made countless foreign policy mistakes because we failed to learn from the past. We have repeated these mistakes in the Middle East, not bothering to ask, "What will the consequences be?" These endless wars in the Middle East have cost trillions of dollars and the lives of American soldiers.

One might ask where were those weapons of mass destruction that the George W. Bush administration claimed Saddam had? The war hawks were eager for war and decapitation of the Iraqi leadership. President George W. Bush's plan failed because he learned nothing from history.

One could add he didn't learn from his own father, President George H. W. Bush, who won the Persian Gulf War, but did not seek regime change in Iraq.

But George W. Bush stayed in Iraq, foolishly thinking we could change hearts and minds and engage in nation building. We were wrong to believe that Iraq wanted to be like a mini U.S. in the desert, promoting democracy and freedom for all. The Iraqi traditions had been already established for thousands of years, and they had no desire to emulate the West. Initially, we were seen as liberators, but soon we became occupiers.

President George W. Bush probably never heard the expression "the devil you know is sometimes better than the devil you don't know." Because the U.S. took out Saddam Hussein, a terrorist group called ISIS filled the void in the Middle East and went on a murderous spree throughout the region, leaving a trail of devastation.

President Joe Biden also forgot the lessons of Vietnam when he abruptly exited Afghanistan. This exit eerily resembled the fall of Saigon. Again, what are the consequences of not studying your history? The answer in this case was thirteen dead American soldiers.

The more I learn about Stoicism, the more I see how it intertwines with our daily lives. On a personal note, I struggled with self-control and discipline in my early years from my teens until my late thirties. I'm now in my fifties. For the last twenty years, I've stopped abusing alcohol. Although I was never a daily drinker, I had a problem. I was haunted by a car accident that I was a passenger in when a friend died. As a Catholic, I pray all the time. I see the benefits of Stoicism and being mindful. I understand what I can control and what I can't. If the problem is too big for me, I give it up to God.

I've also encountered difficult people who constantly speak ill of others. I try to avoid these people at all costs, so I don't get dragged into negativity. I'm careful with how I react to situations and try to keep my emotions in check. In my mind, I try to think of myself as a lion tamer. I'm whipping back those emotions and biting my tongue, practicing self-control and discipline.

Work has always been a kind of experimental laboratory where you can practice your Stoic principles. You have to be disciplined, focus on your task, and block out the noise. I'm reminded of Bill Belichick, one of the most successful football coaches of all time. While he never claimed to be a Stoic, he certainly practiced some of its principles. His emotions were in check, which helped him make the best decisions for his football team. He was unfazed by ridicule and focused only on the actions he could control. After a game, Belichick would turn the page and tell the press, "We are now off to Buffalo and will prepare for that team." His demeanor remained the same in both victories or defeats, except when he won six Super Bowls as a head coach, when he showed his joy. Embracing adversity and welcoming challenges have motivated me, but Stoicism has taught me that events will unfold as they are meant to. So I try not to stress and just do the best I can.

I also appreciated listening to Steve Jobs' commencement speech at Stanford. Jobs discussed how he dropped out of Reed College and accepted his circumstances. He believed in following his passion rather than being swayed by external factors. When he was fired from Apple, he persevered and later was rehired and created products that are widely used across the world. What struck me most was he understood that life's journey was about connecting the dots, that he learned from his failures and his struggles, and it all made sense to him. His passion for his work resonates with Stoic principles for living a life of purpose.[110]

As for Admiral Stockdale's courage, leadership, and sacrifice, he will continue to inspire future generations. His experiences are extreme, no doubt, but they are good lessons for us to think about as we journey through life. A true Stoic knows that nothing external can shatter one's spirit because we are in control of our own thoughts.

Technology, AI, and the Brave New World

"Where we are going there are no roads," said Dr. Emmett Brown in the movie *Back to the Future*. Technology has taken off since that iconic 1985 film was made, but we still have roads. The question is whether we are behind the steering wheel—or if there will even be a steering wheel at all?

By 2035, I envision the transportation landscape will have been transformed completely. Full self-driving is the future whether you like it or not, and car ownership as we know it will have vanished. In my opinion, we will be hailing these cars on our phones or watches.

We will be able to kick back and relax, watch TV, do our homework, or take a nap in these robotaxis. This will be equivalent to flying in a plane, culminating in arriving at your destination courteous of technology, avoiding traffic, and, most importantly, getting there in one piece. Rest assured, the government will have the statistics to prove that robotaxis are safer than an individual driving an automobile. The wizardry of the future technology is soon to be upon us in this transition to self-driving cars. I, for one, look forward to my daughter never having to drive a car and arriving at her destination safely each time. What a relief that will be!

I'm also looking forward to having a robot help with my yard. It could push or drive the lawnmower or trim my hedges and take care of other household duties like laundry—now that would be great. A robot from Tesla and Optimus Prime would suffice, and it's coming soon. I expect the robot wave to hit neighborhoods by 2030, and who knows, the price might even be lower than I expect, perhaps $15,000 to $20,000. These technologies need chips to power the AI boom, and companies like Nvidia are leading the way.

I remember walking through my college campus in 1993, and no one had a cell phone. During this time, I sent my first email from a computer lab, not knowing how the whole process worked. I also recall taking a communication class in which the teacher discussed the "Information Highway" and how it would be much easier to communicate on a variety of levels in the future.

I grew up with Atari playing Pac-Man, and as kids, we would also go to our local convenience store, pop a quarter in an arcade game, and play Donkey Kong and Spy Hunter and have a blast. Our biggest concern was leaving our bikes out in front of the store because one might get stolen. We were collectors of baseball cards and would make a ten- to fifteen-mile trek on our bikes to score a card. Today, if I want that baseball card, I just order it on Amazon. If I want to play a video game, I can just play it on my phone. If I want to watch a movie, I don't have to go to a Blockbuster; I can just stream it. These technological changes happened over time, but with AI, greater innovation will come quicker than you will ever imagine. You are living in a Brave New World!

The need to go into the office has been slowly dying, and we got a taste of what the future will look like staying home and working. I believe that future technology will make you feel like you are in the office with virtual reality. Fighting wars using robots is not as far-fetched as you think. Drones can be operated thousands of miles from the war zone and can inflict severe damage on the battlefield. Companies like Palantir and other AI technologies can strategize and implement best practices in warfare. We might finally achieve President Reagan's dream of Star Wars or the Strategic Defense Initiative, intercepting nuclear missiles launched against the United States and shooting them down with laser technology. The Layered Laser Defense (LLD) system developed by Lockheed Martin has the potential to protect America from a nuclear strike. This technology has already shown the ability to defeat cruise missiles and drones.[111]

Medical devices such as Neuralink are designed to help people with disabilities by implanting tiny electrodes into the brain. This device can help those with quadriplegia and spinal cord injuries control prosthetic limbs using their thoughts, and it can help the blind see through visual cortex stimulation.[112]

I'm also excited about space exploration and the prospect of settling a colony on Mars. I'm certain SpaceX and NASA will be on the forefront of new discoveries in our universe. I believe that first contact with other planets could come sooner than we expect. With AI machine learning and analyzing data, combined with advancements in telescope technology like the James Webb Telescope, who knows what we'll discover? I think AI will speed the process of first contact, raising the question: are we ready for it?

Back in 1977, two probes were launched: Voyager 1 and Voyager 2. They are now in interstellar space. Both these probes carry a golden record that contains messages, images, and sounds from Earth, just in case an alien finds our spacecraft and wants to get in touch with us. It should be noted that our smartphones have more technology than these probes have. Regardless, the Voyager missions have accomplished much and have sent back important data from beyond our solar system.

You can only imagine what a Voyager 3 probe would be outfitted with, but it certainly would have an advanced form of the golden record. Voyager 3 would have the latest AI advanced technology and the ability for advanced mapping of interstellar space, with higher-speeds communication and cameras capable of capturing high-resolution images and sending them back to Earth promptly. Voyager 3 could have robots on board conducting valuable experiments. The future certainly looks interesting, and I hope I'm around to see these new technologies take hold.

Edward M. Kennedy, The Death of Dreams

Heraclitus of Ephesus wrote, "A man's character is his fate."

Every individual weaves a narrative of who they are and how they fit into this world. Of course, people want to present themselves in the best light possible. But like people, events can be inherently flawed. Some events withstand close scrutiny, while others unravel like a cascade of lies and deception—case in point, Chappaquiddick.

In the late 1960s, the American people wanted to believe that one last hope remained. They hoped that Senator Edward Kennedy, commonly referred to as "Ted," would carry the torch for a generation left unfulfilled. But the dreams of reclaiming Camelot perished with the death of Mary Jo Kopechne.

Although this tragic incident became the death knell for the prospect of a Ted Kennedy presidency, it unleashed a "Lion in the Senate" who roared for almost forty-seven years on the national political stage.

Senator Kennedy booked a hotel room at the Shiretown Inn for July 18 and 19, 1969, because he planned to compete in the Forty-third annual Edgartown Yacht Club Regatta in Martha's Vineyard. His cousin and advisor Joseph Gargan and Paul Markham, a former United States Attorney General of Massachusetts, were planning to serve as Kennedy's crew. Kennedy's boat, the *Victura*, finished a dismal ninth place that day.

The weekend was not just about boat racing—it was also supposed be a reunion for six female assistants known as the "Boiler Room Girls" who were all in their twenties and who had worked for the late Robert Kennedy in his quest for the presidency. A beach cottage had been rented to host the reunion party for that weekend on Chappaquiddick island, which was a very short ferry ride from Edgartown.

Ted Kennedy's male assistants were also going be in attendance. However, wives were not invited to Chappaquiddick that weekend. Ted Kennedy's pregnant wife Joan was at home on bed rest because of her two previous miscarriages. Joan later had a third miscarriage and blamed it on what happened at Chappaquiddick.

The reunion of the Boiler Room Girls dredged up feelings of what could have been if Robert F. Kennedy had survived. Now the Boiler Room Girls were being asked to look toward the likelihood of a Ted Kennedy run for president. Their help and loyalty would be needed to secure a Kennedy victory.

On that Friday night of July 18, an accident occurred that derailed Ted Kennedy's political path and ended the life of twenty-eight-year-old Mary Jo Kopechne.

The account that Senator Kennedy gave of that particular evening of the party was that Mary Jo fell ill and he decided to take her back to the hotel room in Edgartown. It was later found out that Mary Jo left her keys and purse at the cottage. This raised a red flag about the Kennedy story. Why would she leave her keys and purse at the cottage if she was returning to her hotel room?

Kennedy said the accident happened on that Friday, July 18, before midnight, but a police officer ending his shift saw a car on the side of the road at 12:40 a.m. on the 19th. The car sped off, and the officer did not pursue it.

The senator alleged he was heading toward the ferry but took a wrong turn. Kennedy's car, a black Oldsmobile, veered off Dike's Bridge into a poucha pond, where Mary Jo Kopechne died. A poucha pond is not in the ocean—it's a tidal pond. Kennedy claimed he dove down multiple times in the murky waters to save her but was unsuccessful.

Kennedy later walked back about a mile to the beach cottage, but at no time did he stop at nearby cottages to ask for help. When he reached the beach cottage where his friends were, he sought the aid of Joseph Garage and Paul Markham, who returned to the scene of the incident with him. They reportedly dove down multiple times, but their attempts to save Mary Jo also failed.

What the senator did next in my opinion was reprehensible—he probably took a rowboat over to Edgartown to his hotel. Kennedy claimed he swam across the channel to his hotel and then waited appropriately ten hours to notify police. Kennedy went on to say that he suffered from shock, exhaustion, and a concussion, and those were the reasons he waited to notify the proper authorities.

This tragedy swiftly turned into a political event, and former Kennedy advisors and fixers were summoned to the Kennedy compound in Hyannis. They were asked to devise a strategy to save what was left of Ted Kennedy's political career.

The senator was charged with leaving the scene of an accident and causing bodily harm. Kennedy's negligent driving was found to be the probable cause of the car accident, but he did not serve any jail time. In April 1970, a grand jury also looked into the case and concluded there was not enough evidence to indict Kennedy on any charges.[113]

As the Ted Kennedy saga unfolded, the nation rapidly turned its attention to achievement of a goal set by the late President John F. Kennedy—landing a man on the moon before the end of the '60s. President Kennedy's speech on September 12, 1962, at Rice University inspired a generation. "We choose to go to the Moon in this decade and do the other things, not because they are easy, but because they are hard." As this lofty dream of the landing on the moon was achieved, back on Earth, Senator Kennedy faced scrutiny that would follow him all the rest of his life.[114]

Senator Kennedy requested television airtime and delivered a political speech taking responsibility for the accident and shooting down rumors that he was drunk or acting inappropriately as a married man. He left it to the voters of Massachusetts and the country to decide if he was telling the truth and if his remorse was genuine.

He might have been forgiven at home in Massachusetts for Chappaquiddick, but the rest of the country was not so kind, thus ending his future presidential ambitions. Senator Kennedy ran for the Democratic nominee for president in 1980 with Chappaquiddick behind him—or so he thought. Those who opposed Kennedy often referred to the Watergate scandal, stating, "Nobody Drowned at Watergate." The controversy clung to Kennedy like an albatross.

Even though the incumbent Jimmy Carter went on to defeat Senator Kennedy, the senator's speech at the Democratic convention was one the best he gave in his political career. It harkened back to his brothers who inspired the country.

"For all those whose cares have been our concern," he said, "the work goes on, the cause endures, the hope still lives, and the dream shall never die."

Despite Chappaquiddick, Ted Kennedy's Massachusetts constituents continued to elect him, making Kennedy the fourth-longest serving senator in United States history.

If people wanted their politicians to be perfect, Mitt Romney would have beaten Ted Kennedy in 1994 in the Massachusetts Senate contest. Romney, a very successful and handsome businessman, seemed to have it all—wealth and the perfect family. This race was Kennedy's biggest challenge for his senate seat.

Clearly, Ted's womanizing and drinking habits were common knowledge. Ted Kennedy's fairly new marriage to Victoria Reggie played a key role in defeating the upstart Republican Mitt Romney. Victoria became a stabilizing force for Ted, something he desperately needed. "Party boy Ted's" days were over.[115]

The Kennedy political ads painted Romney as a corporate raider or a vulture capitalist who took over companies and slashed people's jobs.

Romney worked for Bain Capital and was the founding chief executive. These political TV ads tipped the scales for Kennedy. All the subtle reminders of Mary Jo's death were enough to secure a Mitt Romney victory, but it was close. The final count was Democrat Ted Kennedy 1,266,011 votes, 58.07%, Republican Mitt Romney 894,005 votes, 41.01%.[116]

Were the people of Massachusetts just so enamored with Kennedy's last name that they glossed over Ted's shortcomings? There's no doubt the Catholic Democrats in Massachusetts, especially the Irish, would support Kennedy come hell or high water. During John F. Kennedy's presidency, many households in New England had his picture hanging next to a crucifix. Massachusetts always proved to be Kennedy country for Ted.

The inconsistencies in people's character can disappoint us, and Senator Edward Kennedy serves as a reminder of our human fallibility. At the same time, he embodied the darker arts of politics by leveraging his connections to escape severe punishment for his actions.

We are all sinners, which raises the question: how do we atone? Atonement involves reflecting upon and acknowledging our wrongs, seeking reconciliation, and taking steps in the right direction to make amends.

> Atonement is a process that never ends. I believe that. Maybe it's a New England thing, or an Irish thing, or a Catholic thing. Maybe all of those things. But it's as it should be.—Senator Ted Kennedy[117]

How did Senator Kennedy atone for his sins? In his Senate career, he accomplished the following.

He cast 15,235 votes.

He authored 2,500 bills.

He cosponsored 552 pieces of legislation. Here are some laws he helped to pass.

Civil Rights Act of 1964

Immigration Act of 1965

Voting Rights Act Extension of 1970

Women, Infants, and Children Nutrition Program of 1972 (WIC)

Civil Rights Commission Act Amendments of 1978

Refugee Act of 1980

Voting Rights Act Amendments of 1982

Civil Rights Restoration Act of 1987

Immigration Act of 1990

Civil Rights Act of 1991

Violence Against Women Act of 1994

No Child Left Behind Act of 2001

Bioterrorism Preparedness Act of 2002

Enhanced Border Security and Visa Reform Act of 2002

Matthew Shepard Local Law Enforcement Hate Crimes Prevention Act of 2007

Civil Rights Act of 2008

Senator Kennedy placed a high priority on health care, which helped earn him his nickname, the "Lion of Senate."

Medical Device Amendments of 1976

Consolidated Omnibus Budget Reconciliation Act (COBRA) of 1985

Protection and Advocacy for Mentally Ill Individuals Act of 1986

Nutrition Labeling and Education Act of 1990

Americans with Disabilities Act of 1990

Ryan White Comprehensive AIDS Resources Emergency Act of 1990 (Ryan White CARE Act)

National Institutes of Health Revitalization Act of 1993

Freedom of Access to Clinic Entrances Act of 1994

Health Insurance Portability and Accountability Act of 1996 (HIPAA)

Food and Drug Administration Modernization Act of 1997

Children's Health Insurance Program (CHIP) in 1997

Healthcare Research and Quality Act of 1999

Children's Health Act of 2000

Minority Health and Health Disparities Research and Education Act of 2001

Project BioShield Act of 2003

Pandemic and All-Hazards Preparedness Act of 2005

Family Opportunity Act of 2006

Minority Health Improvement and Health Disparity Elimination Act of 2006

FDA Amendments Act of 2007

Genetic Information Nondiscrimination Act of 2008[118]

Did he escape severe punishment at Chappaquiddick by skillfully navigating the situation by lying and using the political system to his advantage? The answer is yes.

Would the country have been better served if Kennedy had gone to jail and been forced to resign? The answer is debatable, but the Catholic faith teaches that faith and works go hand in hand. Our faith inspires good deeds, and good deeds strengthen our faith. Senator Kennedy can be an example of one who has failed in his personal life but partakes in good works, helping others by passing over 2,000 pieces of legislation.

Kennedy went on to live a full life with Victoria Reggie at his side. He sailed his boat with his grandchildren and worked tirelessly in the Senate. Ted Kennedy never become president, and some will argue that is his punishment. But perhaps his real punishment was living with the guilt of his actions.

Senator Kennedy was diagnosed with malignant glioma in May 2008 and passed away at his home in Hyannis home at the age of seventy-seven on August 25, 2009.

In July before he succumbed to his illness, Ted Kennedy wrote a letter to Pope Benedict XVI that President Obama hand-delivered at the Vatican.

Most Holy Father,

I asked President Obama to personally hand deliver this letter to you. As a man of deep faith himself, he understands how important my Roman Catholic faith is to me and I am so deeply grateful to him. I hope this letter finds you in good health. I pray that you have all of God's blessings as you lead our church and inspire our world during challenging times.

I am writing with deep humility to ask that you pray for me as my own health declines. I was diagnosed with brain cancer over a year ago and although I am undergoing treatment, the disease is taking its toll on me.

I am 77-years-old and preparing for the next passage of life. I've been blessed to be part of a wonderful family and both my parents, specifically my mother, kept our Catholic faith at the center of our lives. That gift of faith has sustained and nurtured and provided solace to me in the darkest hours. I know that I have been an imperfect human being, but with the help of my faith I have tried to right my past.

I want you to know, your Holiness, that in my 50 years of elected office I have done my best to champion the rights of the poor and open doors of economic opportunity. I've worked to welcome the immigrant, to fight discrimination and expand access to health care and education. I've opposed the death penalty and fought to end war. Those are the issues that have motivated me and have been the focus of my work as a U.S. Senator.

I also want you to know that even though I am ill, I am committed to do everything I can to achieve access to healthcare for everyone in my country. This has been the political cause of my life. I believe in a conscience protection for Catholics in the health field and I'll continue to advocate for it as my colleagues in the Senate and I work to develop an overall national health policy that guarantees health care for everyone. I've always tried to be a faithful Catholic, Your Holiness. And though I have fallen short through human failings I've never failed to believe and respect the fundamental teachings of my faith.

I continue to pray for God's blessings on you and on our church and would be most thankful for your prayers for me.

The pope's assistant replied:

The Holy Father has read the letter in which you entrusted to President Obama, who kindly presented it to him during his recent meeting.

He was saddened to know of your illness and asked me to assure you of his concern and his spiritual closeness. He is particularly grateful of your prayers for him and for the needs of our universal church. His Holiness prays that in the days ahead you may be sustained in faith and hope and granted the precious grace of joyful surrender to the will of God, our merciful Father.

He invokes upon you the consolation and peace of our risen savior, to all who share in his sufferings and trust in his promise of eternal life, commending you and the members of your family to the loving intervention of the Blessed Virgin Mary.

The Holy Father cordially imparts his apostolic blessing as a pledge of wisdom, comfort and strength in the Lord.[119]

Ted Kennedy wrote in his memoir *True Compass*, "That night on Chappaquiddick Island ended in a horrible tragedy that haunts me every day of my life. I had suffered sudden and violent loss far too many times, but this night was different. This night I was responsible. It was an accident, but I was responsible."

As I wrote this essay, I felt a deep sadness in my heart for Mary Jo. She was an afterthought for many when we think about this tragedy. She was just the girl in the car who died when Ted Kennedy drove off the bridge.

I think about Mary Jo's poor parents and their lost dreams. Mary Jo would never get married and experience the joy of having her own family. It all ended at Chappaquiddick for her in a murky Poucha Pond.

We can only pray and hope that in her despair as she slowly drowned, she escaped the darkness as God held her in the palms of his hands during her final moments.

Elvis Presley, A World without a King

Nothing Gold Can Stay

By Robert Frost

Nature's first green is gold,
Her hardest hue to hold.
Her early leaf's a flower;
But only so an hour.
Then leaf subsides to leaf.
So Eden sank to grief,
So dawn goes down to day.
Nothing gold can stay.

Elvis Presley was born in Tupelo, Mississippi, on January 8, 1935. When he was thirteen, he moved to Memphis, Tennessee, and lived in public housing. No one thought this boy would grow up to be a superstar. A cloud hung over Elvis, the loss of his stillborn twin brother, Jesse Garon Presley. This tragedy had a profound impact on Elvis and his entire family. Elvis' mother believed that "when one twin died, the other that lived got all the strength of both."[120]

Elvis' father once said, "Of course, Elvis and I both wondered over the years whether his life would have been drastically different had his brother lived. I've concluded that it wouldn't have been because I believe Elvis' career and contribution to the world were fated from the first. For during his early life, certain things happened which convinced me that God had given my wife and me a very special child for whom He had some very special plans."[121]

I believe the loss of his twin was a significant force behind Elvis and his pursuit of success. Sometimes, profound losses can drive us forward. When I think of Elvis, I can't help but reflect on the poem by Robert Frost, whose words capture for me Elvis' greatness, but also his end. The first part of Elvis' career was like a rocket shooting to the moon and how he graced the stage with talent that was simply beyond comprehension, taking the world by storm. But nothing gold can stay, and over time, watching his body and health wilt away right before our eyes, you understand clearly the harshness of life. The light eventually went out on the King, and we were robbed of seeing the full extent of Elvis' creativity and the future magic he could have displayed on the stage.

Although the curtain fell sooner than we wished, history teaches us that true greatness stands the test of time. Consider William Shakespear and his splendid works, *Romeo and Juliet* and *Hamlet*; Leonardo da Vinci, who created masterpieces like the *Mona Lisa* and the *Last Supper*; and Elvis Presley, the King of Rock and Roll, who sold an estimated one billion records worldwide and had eighteen number one hits on the Billboard 100.

1. Heartbreak Hotel (1956)
2. I Want You, I Need You, I Love You (1956)
3. Don't Be Cruel (1956)
4. Hound Dog (1956)
5. Love Me Tender (1956)
6. Too Much (1957)

7. All Shook Up (1957)

8. (Let Me Be Your) Teddy Bear (1957)

9. Jailhouse Rock (1957)

10. Don't (1958)

11. Hard-headed Woman (1958)

12. A Big Hunk o'Love (1959)

13. Stuck on You (1960)

14. It's Now or Never (1960)

15. Are You Lonesome Tonight? (1960)

16. Surrender (1961)

17. Good Luck Charm(1962)

18. Suspicious Minds (1969)

Elvis' awards were also abundant.

1960: Star on the Hollywood Walk of Fame

1968: Variety Star from the Photoplay Awards

1970: Nominated for Entertainer of the Year by the Academy of Country Music

1971: Nominated for Album of the Year for *Moody Blue* by the Academy of Country Music

1971: Won a Grammy for Best Inspirational Performance for "He Touched Me"

1971: Won a Grammy Lifetime Achievement at age 36

1973: Won a Grammy for Best Inspirational Performance for "How Great Thou Art"

1977: Won a Gold Medal for Favorite Variety Star from the Photoplay Awards

1986: Inducted into the Rock and Roll Hall of Fame

1987: Won the Award of Merit from the American Music Awards

1998: Inducted into the Country Music Hall of Fame

2008: Star from the Music City Walk of Fame[122]

Elvis also starred in thirty-one movies, including *Love Me Tender, Loving You, Jailhouse Rock, King Creole,* and *Viva Las Vegas.* Although Hollywood didn't fully recognize his acting talents, Elvis' musical abilities were extraordinary. Never had there been a musical talent quite like Elvis Presley. He was a phenomenal showman, scoring hit after hit. Not only could he dance and sing, but he could also play the piano, drums, bass, ukulele, and accordion. Elvis was the definition of electrifying and was deeply influenced by his Southern roots and gospel background.[123]

There was certainly more to Elvis than the average person knew. He was quite generous, often helping people, sometimes strangers, out of the blue. There are stories of him helping people broken down on the side of the road by having their car towed and then buying them a brand-new one. His philanthropy was impressive; he made appearances to benefit charities, put on free concerts to raise money, and lent his name to causes like the March of Dimes, the American Cancer Society, the American Library Association, the USS *Arizona* Memorial, and St. Jude's Children's Hospital. Elvis would donate $100,000 a year to each of fifty charitable organizations. There are stories of him buying Cadillacs for his friends and random people and paying off mortgages.[124]

Let's not forget the significant role Elvis played in the Civil Rights Movement and his impact as a change agent in history. Elvis deeply respected black musicians and singers such as Arthur Crudup, Little Richard, James Brown, Ray Charles, Big Mama Thornton, and Ike Turner. During the tumultuous times of racial segregation, Elvis helped bridge the divide with race relations. In the 1950s and 1960s, he made a significant impact with his music, bringing African American music into the mainstream. Like millions of Americans, Elvis was distraught when Dr. King was assassinated on April 4, 1968, at the Lorraine Motel in Memphis, Tennessee ,and then two months later when Bobby Kennedy was killed on June 5, 1968, at the Ambassador Hotel in Los Angeles, California. Elvis hosted a Christmas special on TV on December 3, 1968, ending it by singing "If I Can Dream." His song captures the moment of sadness and attempts to unite the country. It is a memorable performance of Elvis in his white suit singing to the broken hearts of Americans who had tragically lost two towering Civil Rights leaders.[125]

I do think the writing was on the wall for Elvis when he covered the song "Unchained Melody" in June 1977, just two months before his death. This song was on the last Elvis Presley album, *Moody Blue*. Watching him on YouTube, I wondered how he would perform this song. He speaks softly, almost incoherently, making a few jokes as he sits down at the piano. This isn't the young Elvis anymore; his appearance had changed dramatically over time, with age and weight playing a part. His once clean-cut look, emphasized by sharp suits and ties from a Memphis tailor shop, Lansky Bros., has been replaced by the Las Vegas trademark look of outlandish outfits with capes, high collars, and rhinestones. At first glance, you'd think Elvis was washed up, but then his voice fills the room, strong and commanding. Elvis masterfully belts out a beautiful rendition of a song that left me emotional as I thought about how close he was to death. As sweat rolls off his face and the song concludes, you realize all his energy was poured into it and his voice that never failed him. I'm left with a sense of amazement, yet at the same time a sensation of being punched in the gut.[126]

It seems like so many great entertainers have met tragic or untimely deaths. Dying peacefully in your sleep of natural causes seems to never be the case. Think of James Dean, an actor Elvis admired for his role in *Rebel Without a Cause*, who perished in a head-on collision in his Porsche 550 Spyder on September 30, 1955, near Cholame, California. Or the day the music died, when young Buddy Holly, at twenty-two, died in a plane crash on February 3, 1959, near Clear Lake, Iowa. Also on board were Ritchie Valens, only seventeen, and J. P. "The Big Bopper" Richardson, twenty-eight.[127]

For Elvis, who had all the great accomplishments and a lavish life full of pomp and circumstance, dying on the bathroom floor at forty-two on August 16, 1977, at Graceland was shocking and almost unseemly for a king. Elvis was found by his fiancée Ginger Alden. Next to his body was a book called *A Scientific Search for the Face of Jesus*, focusing on the Shroud of Turin. Elvis spent his last moments seeking solace in spirituality amid a life spiraling out of control.[128]

If you were alive the day Elvis died, you doubtless remember where you were or how you found out about his death. The president at the time, Jimmy Carter, made a statement that struck at the heart of how much Elvis meant to the nation.

> Elvis Presley's death deprives our country of a part of itself. He was unique and irreplaceable. More than 20 years ago, he burst upon the scene with an impact that was unprecedented and will probably never be equaled. His music and his personality, fusing the styles of white country and black rhythm and blues, permanently changed the face of American popular culture.[129]

Frank Sinatra, who was a harsh critic of Elvis early on, eventually came around and a friendship blossomed. Upon hearing about Elvis' death, Sinatra said, "There have been many accolades uttered about Elvis' talent and performances through the years, all of which I agree with wholeheartedly. I shall miss him dearly as a friend. He was a warm, considerate and generous man."[130]

Over 30,000 people were let into Graceland for a public viewing, and the estate was covered with thousands of flower arrangements sent by adoring fans. Hollywood stars and rock legends traveled to Graceland to pay their respects, including Frank Sinatra, George Hamilton, Burt Reynolds, John Wayne, and Ann-Margret. The Godfather of Soul, James Brown, was the only entertainer given special permission by Vernon Presley, Elvis' father, to see Elvis in his casket. James said of Elvis, "I wasn't just a fan, I was his brother. The last time I saw Elvis alive was at Graceland. We sang 'Old Blind Barnabas' together, a gospel song. I love him and hope to see him in heaven. There'll never be another like that soul brother."

The sermon was held in the living room at Graceland on August 18, 1977, by Pastor C. W. Bradley from Wooddale Church of Christ. Jackie Kahane, a comedian who opened for Elvis, gave a testimonial. J. D. Sumner and the Stamps, the Statesmen, and Kathy Westmoreland performed "Heavenly Father," a favorite hymn of the King. Sixteen white limousines carrying mourners and family members, followed a white 1977 Miller-meteor Landau traditional Cadillac hearse carrying Elvis' body as it traveled from Graceland to Forest Cemetery, where Elvis was buried next to his mother. Both their graves were relocated in October of that same year to Graceland Meditation Garden because of an attempt to steal Elvis' body.[131]

As estimated 80,000 to 100,000 visibly upset fans, old and young, lined both sides of the street. Elvis, who stirred all sorts of emotions within his fans when he was performing, in his death had devastated them. Indeed, the United States and the world grieved in unison. Fans mourned Elvis' death as if they personally knew him because his music was a part of their lives. Just weeks before, a tell-all book had been published in which three of his former bodyguards had depicted Elvis as addicted to drugs and behaving erratically. Fans of the King glued the pages of the book shut at public libraries across the nation.[132]

In her posthumous memoir *From Here to the Great Unknown*, which was completed by her daughter Riley Keough, Elvis' daughter Lisa Marie Presley gives us an inside glimpse of the King's life and family struggles. Lisa Marie was nine when her father passed away. She revealed her constant worry about him dying. "Sometimes I'd see him and he was out of it. Sometimes I would find him passed out. I wrote a poem with the line, 'I hope my daddy doesn't die.'" Her fear was real as Elvis' life was out of control. The divorce from Priscilla compounded his troubles, sending him into a four-year tailspin from which he never recovered. Elvis' daughter also struggled with prescription drug addiction. She passed away at the age of fifty-four due to complications from a small bowel obstruction.[133]

Elvis died of a heart attack, with his official cause of death listed as cardiac arrhythmia. The full medical report will be released in 2027 because of Tennessee privacy laws. However, it was reported he had ten different drugs in his system, although they were not deemed directly responsible for his death: phenobarbital, butobarbital, codeine morphine, methaqualone, diazepam (valium), N-desmethyldiazepam (nordazepam), ethinamate, ethchlorvynol (placidyl), and pentobarbital.[134]

Elvis Presley also had an interesting diet that some would say was not healthy. Elvis would sometimes eat the Fool Gold Loaf, which was a jar of blueberry jam, an entire pound of bacon, and a jar of peanut butter. It was made with a stick of butter, a total of 8,000 calories.[135]

Other foods Elvis ate that weren't especially healthy were peanut butter and banana sandwiches, party meatballs, classic fried breakfast, hot dogs with sauerkraut, BBQ bologna seasoned with vinegar, red pepper, lemon juice, and salt, Harvard Texas caviar, cheeseburgers, Spanish omelet, sugar-glazed salmon, fried pickles, fried chicken, meatloaf, mac and cheese prepared the Southern way, sweet potato pie, milkshakes, chocolate chip cookies, jelly donuts, M&Ms, ice cream bars, and coconut cake.[136]

Elvis was reportedly hospitalized four times before his death with mild diabetes, liver problems, hypertension, and an enlarged colon. Elvis also suffered from glaucoma and constipation. His diet, the prescription drugs, and poor management contributed to his health problems.

Elvis' manager, Colonel Tom Parker, had a shady past. Parker, whose real name was Andreas Cornelius van Kuijk, was born in Breda, Netherlands, in 1909, and entered the United States illegally at age twenty. Parker served in the United States Army and was court-martialed for desertion. He spent time in a military prison before being released with a diagnosis of psychopathic personality disorder. Parker worked in the carnival and music promotion industries and met Elvis on February 6, 1955, in a cafe called Palumbo's in Memphis, Tennessee.[137]

Having Colonel Parker as his manager was a double-edged sword. Parker promoted the hell out of Elvis, but simultaneously worked him to the bone and ignored his health problems. Parker also used Las Vegas as his own playground, gambling money he didn't have while Elvis performed 641 shows from 1969 to 1976, including a run of fifty-eight consecutive sold-out shows. Elvis stayed in the penthouse suite, Room 3000, at the International Hotel while performing in Las Vegas. On December 12, 1976, Elvis Presley said so long to Vegas in his final performance at the Las Vegas Hilton, which was formerly called the International Hotel. Unaware that death was approaching, Elvis performed for the last time at Market Square Arena in Indianapolis on June 26, 1977. His final song was "Can't Help Falling in Love with You."[138]

Elvis' death still leaves fans feeling sad and wondering why no one took a real hard stance against his lifestyle, especially when he was spiraling downward right before their eyes. Why did most of his friends and family and his fiancée Ginger Alden just continue with business as usual, thinking, "Well, that's the way it is"? Some might say it was much more complicated than that. He was his own man, determined to do what he wanted. But in the throes of depression and prescription drugs as he was, one questions how much control Elvis had over anything in that last year.[139]

What can we learn from Elvis, his life and his death? First, true rags to riches stories can happen, and Elvis was proof of that. Perhaps there is a hidden star in America living in poverty that is just waiting to break out and become the next big thing. It says something about America that despite hardships, you can rise up and claim a piece of the American dream. Even after Elvis' tragic death, his music flourished and lives on, with his songs constantly playing on the radio and celebrated in 1950s diners across America.

Elvis' death hurts us more because it was largely self-inflicted, but remember addiction is a disease, and he needed professional treatment to get better. Our medical experience in this field has improved since the 1970s, but as a country, we still need to do better. For those who have suffered with addictions, you can only imagine how difficult it is to overcome a disease of drugs or alcohol, especially when fame is added to the mix. If Elvis had the chance to reflect and recover with therapy, he might have lived another forty years or more.

We have a prescription drug problem in America that doesn't seem to be getting any better. There were an estimated 107, 543 drug overdose deaths in the United States during 2023. Also, in our nation, there were approximately 261 alcohol-related deaths each day. It doesn't look like we have learned any lessons since the King's death. It is also unfortunate that we have lost many stars to addiction, and it seems that history keeps repeating itself time and time again.

We wish that Elvis' life had turned out differently. We think that if we could only turn back the hands on the clock, maybe we could have saved him. But we know this is a futile exercise. We cannot change the past, but we can embrace the love that flowed from it. With Elvis, we are left with beautiful music that means so much to people around the world.

Our hearts will forever be broken.

The U.S. Debt, The Next Black Swan

One could argue that those aspiring to the presidency of the United States should be required to read George Washington's 1796 Farewell Address. Some might feel it is an out-of-touch document that bears no significance to modern-day America because the speech was given in a very different time and place in our history.

The country has increased dramatically in population from a mere four million since Washington's time to 337 million now. Of course, industry and technology have advanced considerably along with the landscape. Still, our American ideals have remained, and Washington's words are still relevant.

Before he gave his famous address, in 1793, Washington said to lawmakers, "No pecuniary consideration is more urgent than the regular redemption and discharge of the public debt: on none can delay, be more injurious, or an economy of time more valuable." Washington understood early on that the country was fragile and that it had to be especially careful about wars and debt. The experiment called America could be over quickly if caution was not taken.[140]

George Washington's Farewell address dealt with many important topics such as national unity, political parties, foreign alliance, education, morality, and constitutional adherence, but one that is often overlooked is Washington's views on maintaining public credit and avoiding public debt. Washington's words helped illuminate a path forward for the country. Of course, he was correct on all his assertions. But some presidents have chosen to ignore Washington's words. The results speak for themselves.[141]

The U.S. debt might not be a crisis you care about, but it should keep you up at night because it is a monster. Opinions vary on what the biggest threat to America is. Some claim climate change, others say future pandemics, and others are adamant that it is a nuclear war. Our US. debt is a national security crisis just lurking out there, ready to pounce and send our entire financial system into chaos. It is an American-made Black Swan—that's right, a crisis we created because we have been extremely reckless since the 2000s with wars in the Middle East, bailouts of Wall Street during the 2008 financial crash, COVID-19 relief money in 2020–2021, rising health-care costs, defense spending, tax cuts, infrastructure projects, unemployment benefits, discretionary spending, rebuilding after natural disasters, and billions owed in treasury securities to China. Needless to say, George Washington would not be proud.

So when do the wheels fall off the wagon? Is it when we hit $40 trillion, $43 trillion, $48 trillion, $52 trillion? Our debt is exploding at a quicker pace in recent months, increasing almost to $1 trillion every 100 days, give or take.[142]

Economists like Les Rubin, who is an entrepreneur, accountant, real estate developer, and the founder MainstreetEconomics.org, has said, "Our country cannot pay its current expenses and debts as they mature, so it borrows endlessly to survive. My friends, that is called a Ponzi scheme—and it will end, no one knows when, but it will, some day. It will end in a crisis, and it will be ugly beyond imagination. Yes, it will be worse than the Great Depression—if we let it happen."[143]

We have become deaf to warnings about U.S. debt. We ignore them like the boy who cried wolf. It has been said many times that the U.S. debt could lead to an economic event like we have never witnessed in our lifetimes, but economists don't know when. Until then, we cross our fingers and hope it is not today, which is not a game plan to get our arms around this problem.

Federal Reserve Chair Jerome Powell said, "The debt is growing faster than the economy, so it is unsustainable."[144]

Historian Niall Ferguson's law states, "Any great power that spends more on debt service than on defense will not stay great for very long."[145]

The debt needs to be addressed in a nonpartisan manner. If it is not, the growing debt will just add to higher rates of inflation and erode the U.S. dollar. Do we address the problem and take responsible steps, or do we kick that debt down the road and watch it unleash severe punishment on our children and grandchildren?[146]

Charlie Munger, Wisdom and Humor

Of all the people in history I would have liked to have met and had a coffee with, it would have been Charlie Munger. He was blessed with a great sense of humor and was a gifted storyteller. His honesty was refreshing, and I guess when you are a billionaire, you can say what you want. I would watch him in interviews at the annual Berkshire Hathaway meeting and just crack up. He was a happy warrior in life, achieving unimaginable success, giving common sense investing tips to the average schmuck like me. But there was much more to this man than being a brilliant investor—he was a teacher and philosopher of sorts. He persevered through some of life's worst moments when many would have quit. Charlie Munger was the definition of success and overcoming obstacles, and that is what draws me to him.

Munger served as the vice chairman of Berkshire Hathaway until his death in 2023 at the age of 99. Berkshire Hathaway is one of the most successful conglomerates of all time, worth a staggering hundreds of billions of dollars.

His family faced the Great Depression, and Charlie witnessed firsthand a society coming undone at the seams from poverty. Munger said about the Great Depression, "It was so extreme that people like you have just no idea what the hell it was like. There was nobody who had any money. The rich people didn't have any money. People would come and beg for a meal at the door."[147]

Later in life, he was divorced and then experienced the devastating loss of his nine-year-old son, Teddy, to leukemia. Nothing, of course, compares to the loss of a child, but Charlie stayed the course and believed in himself. One of Charlie Munger's famous quotes, "You can cry but you can't quit," resonated with me because many give up on themselves and their dreams. Munger also said something that struck me because it showed his resilience: "Never feel sorry for yourself…and if your child is dying of cancer, don't feel sorry for yourself, never ever feel sorry for yourself." Munger believed that self-pity should always be avoided and instead that we should focus on what can be done to improve the situation. Charlie also lost his vision in one eye because of a failed cataract operation.[148]

I think Munger was a mentally strong giant, and of course he had his moments of despair, but he kept pressing forward. His life changed when he met Warren Buffet in 1959 at a cocktail party in Omaha, Nebraska, and they exchanged ideas on investing strategies. Munger, who at the time was a successful lawyer in California, established a law firm, Munger, Tolles, & Olson. In 1978, Munger joined Berkshire Hathaway as vice chairman, and the rest, as they say, is history.[149]

I'm sure many of you have overcome some adversity, perhaps even more devastating than what Charlie Munger went through. The point, I guess, is that you have to get up off the mat and keep fighting, as hard as it is. If Munger had quit during his tough times, he would never become one of the best investors of all time. His net worth was $2.5 billion.[150]

On a personal note, I can relate to Charlie Munger and some of the devastating events he experienced in his life. My ex-wife passed away, and I had to support my son through some very difficult days. When I was younger, I was involved in a terrible car accident when my female friend was driving. This accident occurred in the morning on the highway when we were cut off and crushed under an eighteen-wheel truck. I escaped with a hand injury that healed over time, but my friend was killed. As a parent now, I understand even more how devastating it was for her family to lose their little girl at the age of seventeen.

Years later, in my late twenties, I had an accident on my mountain bike, falling and slamming into a rock. It collapsed my lung and almost killed me. Less than a year later, with a two-year-old son, I went through a divorce that felt like a death to me. Being a fairly new father and trying to figure out how to make it work for my son was challenging.

Sometimes the deck just seems to be stacked against us, and we aren't catching a break. The question is, how do we navigate these difficult days that could turn into weeks or in some cases years? There might be no solution or answer to your problem at the moment. Whatever the issue is, we have to be honest with ourselves and ask if we've done all we could.

Life often throws us challenges that can feel overwhelming. Mike Tyson famously said, "Everyone has a plan until we get punched in the face." When things go awry, will our plan hold up? For me, faith has been a cornerstone through troubled times, along with the unwavering support of family and friends. This was in a sense my recipe when things go wrong.

In the last five years, I've also incorporated some of Munger's life-navigating skills in to my own toolkit. Munger's problem-solving and crisis manager abilities offer a way of thinking that can benefit anyone.

A wise friend, a priest, once told me, "Sometimes all you can do is pray, especially when you have exhausted all resources. You might be spinning your wheels looking for answers that other people aren't ready for yet." This advice came to mind when I was debating with my son about the value of a college degree. Despite many walks and talks, we were at odds. I did feel a glimmer of hope that he was listening because he continued to walk with me. We once drove to Walden Pond in Concord, Massachusetts, hoping to summon the spirits of Walden and Thoreau. I thought this would be the moment my son would see the light on the path around Walden Pond. Instead, it poured rain. Actually, it was more like a monsoon, which ended our discussions on college for a few months. My son's civil disobedience seemed to be winning out. At this point, I finally gave it to God because I felt I was getting nowhere. If he had chosen a trade, I would have supported him 100%, but he was lost and at a crossroads.

To my surprise, my son decided to enroll in college a year later and is on the road to graduating. Interestingly, around the same time, I started to familiarize myself with Charlie Munger's ideas and began implementing them at home and work. My strategy now in life is faith, family, and some of Charlie Munger's wisdom.

Munger had a unique way of looking at problems shaped by his experiences. He had an unconventional educational path that, in hindsight, led to his success. Born in Omaha, Nebraska, in 1942, Charlie studied mathematics at the University of Michigan for about a year before dropping out to serve in the military. He then studied meteorology during World War II at Caltech after scoring high on his Army General Classification Test. From 1943–1945, Munger's job in the military was to predict weather patterns for pilots so they didn't crash. This is when he created his inversion thinking strategy.[151]

Munger said, "When I was a meteorologist in World War II, they told me how to draw weather maps and predict the weather. What I was actually doing was clearing pilots to take flights. I just reversed the problem. I inverted, I said: 'Suppose I want to kill a lot of pilots. What would be the easy way to do it?' And I soon concluded that the only easy way to do it was to get the planes into icing conditions they couldn't handle or to get the pilot into a place where he'd run out of fuel before he could safely land. So I made up my mind I was going to stay miles away from killing pilots by either icing or getting them sucked into conditions where they couldn't land."[152]

Hence the phrase that Charlie Munger would repeat over the years: "Always invert."

You can apply the inversion method to investing, your job, or personal life. For example:

How could I lose all my money investing?

How could I get fired from my job?

How could I ruin the relationship I'm in?

You can practice inversion basically on anything, and it should work. Regardless of what business you are in—real estate, investing, or owning a business—the lesson is to pause and avoid recklessness.

Charlie Munger strongly believed in recognizing your own limitations. He often asked, "What is your circle of competence?" It's crucial not to pretend to know something you don't. Munger also emphasized that life and career sometimes don't go as planned. The key is to stay focused and act rationally. For example, when you see your stock portfolio decline, remember that this is a part of the game. Munger also discussed specialization in the workforce, ensuring that others need your skills. Investing in one's self is the best choice, whether that be a college degree or a trade certificate. Munger was also an avid reader and knew about many different topics, making him a uniquely gifted individual. Reading expands your knowledge, which certainly aided Munger in his work.[153]

I think we all have struggled with working with difficult people, and there is no easy answer to that. I'm reminded that the only person you can control is yourself. Navigating workplace politics and understanding the hierarchy are things we all need to figure out sooner or later. You will encounter colleagues who think they are experts but know very little. Your fellow employees or bosses may get frazzled and create unnecessary chaos at work. In these situations, I channel Charlie Munger and stay focused and do the best job possible. Work can be full of landmines, so just try to avoid them and remember Charlie telling you to always invert.

You can also learn from Charlie Munger that success is not just about personal gain, but also about contributing to society and helping others. Charlie Munger donated more than $500 million to schools and universities. His sense of giving back to education and understanding how important it is in society makes me appreciate him even more.[154]

You might be asking what about investing. What were Charlie Munger's secrets? He would never tell you particulars but would offer broad advice. One such example is when Munger stressed the importance of having $100K invested in the market. Munger said, "It's a bitch, but you gotta do it, I don't care what you have to do—if it means walking everywhere and not eating anything that wasn't purchased with a coupon, find a way to get your hands on $100,000." There's a reason why Charlie Munger gave this advice—that $100k threshold is a milestone for the average investor. If you invested at a modest 5% return, and just leave your investments alone for 21 years, not adding a dime, some estimates have that $100k growing to $278,596. Remember, compound interest is the eighth wonder of the world, and over time, it is a powerful force for gaining financial freedom.[155]

Once we realize that being successful requires acknowledging that the future is coming for us whether we like it or not, then we must prepare.

Although nothing is easy and the real world can feel like we're getting hit by a two-by-four, we have to navigate and strategize about our future.

Lastly, Charlie Munger gave old age a good name. His wit, sharpness, and charisma remained intact until the very end. Charlie Munger was a trailblazer not just in investing, but also in thinking and problem-solving. Charlie suffered immensely from the loss of a son, an eye, and a divorce, and he could have given up multiple times, but he found a way forward.

Thank you, Charlie!

I will leave you with a few of his quotes.

My game in life was always to avoid all standard ways of failing. You teach me the wrong way to play poker and I will avoid it. You teach me the wrong way to do something else, I will avoid it. And, of course, I've avoided a lot, because I'm so cautious.[156]

Crazy is way more common than you think, It's easy to slip into crazy. Just avoid it, avoid it, avoid it.[157]

If you rise in life, you have to behave in a certain way. You can go to a strip club if you're a beer-swilling sand shoveler, but if you're the bishop of Boston, you shouldn't go.[158]

Good ideas, carried to wretched excess, become bad ideas. Nobody's gonna say I got some s*** that I want to sell you. They say—it's blockchain![159]

All I want to know is where I'm going to die, so I'll never go there.[160]

Queen of Heaven

When my ex-wife died suddenly of an asthma attack, leaving behind our son and her two daughters from her fairly new marriage, life changed abruptly. At the age of sixteen, my son moved in with me permanently. I was remarried with a two-year-old daughter at the time and thought to myself how fragile life is. It gave me anxiety thinking about my son and his half- sisters losing a parent in a world where you drastically need both.

I leaned on my faith during this time and prayed that my son would be watched over in heaven not just by his mother but also by Mary, the Mother of God.

Mary, the "New Eve," has always offered us a path to escape the darkness through her son Jesus Christ. We must remember that Mary's path had her own trials and triumphs because she was chosen by God to bear the Savior, Lord Jesus Christ.

The Angel Gabriel was sent to give Mary the news that would change her life and the world.

> Luke 1:26-38
> GOD'S WORD Translation
> **The Angel Gabriel Comes to Mary**
> **26** Six months after Elizabeth had become pregnant, God sent the angel Gabriel to Nazareth, a city in Galilee. **27** The angel went to a virgin promised in marriage to a descendant of David named Joseph. The virgin's name was Mary.
> **28** When the angel entered her home, he greeted her and said, "You are favored by the Lord! The Lord is with you."
> **29** She was startled by what the angel said and tried to figure out what this greeting meant.
> **30** The angel told her,

"Don't be afraid, Mary. You have found favor with God.
31 You will become pregnant, give birth to a son, and name him Jesus.
32 He will be a great man and will be called the Son of the Most High. The Lord God will give him the throne of his ancestor David.
33 Your son will be king of Jacob's people forever, and his kingdom will never end."
34 Mary asked the angel, "How can this be? I'm a virgin."
35 The angel answered her, "The Holy Spirit will come to you, and the power of the Most High will overshadow you. Therefore, the holy child developing inside you will be called the Son of God.
36 "Elizabeth, your relative, is six months pregnant with a son in her old age. People said she couldn't have a child.
37 But nothing is impossible for God."
38 Mary answered, "I am the Lord's servant. Let everything you've said happen to me."
Then the angel left her.[161]

Mary's acceptance of God's will serve as a perfect example as we face our own challenges, whether it's sickness, a loss of a loved one, or some cross that we feel is too heavy to carry. Being the second mother to humanity, Mary reminds us that God has a plan, and His love will see us through.

Seven years ago on a warm day in November, I anxiously waited for my son to come home from school. It happened to be a day he was visiting with me during the week. I prayed and sought the strength of Jesus before he arrived so I could deliver the news of his Mom's sad passing. I wondered how my son would ever recover from this loss.

In the years that have followed, I transformed the very spot on the lawn of where I delivered this sad news with vibrant flowers and a pine tree encircled by a bed of mulch. But most importantly, I created a shrine to Mary , the Blessed Mother, turning our grief over to hope. Now every time my son walks up to my front door he can be reminded that he is never alone and always loved

 At the age twenty-three, my son is doing well. Thank God!

Forgiveness

> The line separating good and evil passes not through states, nor between classes, nor between political parties either—but right through every human heart.—Aleksandr Solzhenitsyn[162]

You might identify parts of yourself in some of the history heroes I have written about. Perhaps you can relate to John Quincy Adams and the grief he felt when his father died, or to Charlie Munger, who lost a child, or to Elvis, who struggled with health issues and prescription drug abuse. Maybe it's Richard Nixon, who grappled with his inner demons.

As someone who loves history, I like to evaluate the entire body of work that an individual has contributed. I also seek out redeeming qualities that supersede their imperfections. As a Catholic, I'm prone to forgive, but Jefferson's ownership of slaves is too hard for me to overlook. I argue that he knew better, and it is bewildering to me.

Our history heroes are only human, after all. It can be an eye-opener as we examine their character flaws and mistakes. Do we dismiss their achievements because of their moral shortcomings? Should we forgive their actions and give them credit for trying to shape history in what they believed was the right direction? In Matthew 6:14, Jesus says, "For if you forgive people their transgressions, your Father in the skies will also forgive you. But if you will not forgive people, then neither will your Father forgive your transgressions."

The question might arise: Why do we have to forgive them in the first place? All we have to do is follow the facts, leave our emotions out of it, and tell the story. Historians might argue that this is their role, but for us mere mortals, it might be hard to separate our emotions from their accomplishments and failures. On a personal level, we all have experienced some insult or injury. Can we figure out how to be okay with it, move forward, and live a productive life? Forgiveness can truly be transformative if we open our hearts and seek it.

We should also remember the importance of forgiving ourselves because we often fall short in life. This might be one of the hardest things we ever do. Continuously replaying our guilt over and over again won't change anything, and we must try to put it to rest instead of being held hostage by our past. I visit the confessional and often feel a sense of comfort, love, and understanding as I seek forgiveness. Some might visit a special place or practice another form of worship to seek their peace. One thing is certain: perfection escapes all of us, and no one's life journey is easy, especially for a History Hero.

---

[1] Kathy Alexander, "Hannah Dustin's Revenge," Legends of America, https://www.legendsofamerica.com/hannah-dustins-revenge/.
[2] *A Week on the Concord and Merrimack Rivers*, https://www.britannica.com/topic/A-Week-on-the-Concord-and-Merrimack-Rivers.
[3] History.com editors, "World War II," https://www.history.com/topics/world-war-ii/world-war-ii-history, October 29, 2009, updated August 7, 2024.
[4] Melissa Chan, "'A Date which Will Live in Infamy.' Read President Roosevelt's Pearl Harbor Address," *Time*, https://time.com/4593483/pearl-harbor-franklin-roosevelt-infamy-speech-attack/December 7, 2016, updated December 6, 2018.
[5] *Quincy* (CA-71), 12/15/43-3/1/46, Record Group 24: Records of the Bureau of Naval Personnel Series: Muster Rolls of U.S. Navy Ships, Stations, and Other Naval Activities, National Archives Catalog, https://catalog.archives.gov/id/192149859?objectPage=36; USS *QUINCY*—War Diary, 5/1-31/44, Record Group 38: Records of the Office of the Chief of Naval Operations, Series: World War II War Diaries, Other Operational Records and Histories, National Archives Catalog, https://catalog.archives.gov/id/78475952; USS *QUINCY*—War Diary, 2/1-29/44, Record Group 38: Records of the Office of the Chief of Naval Operations, Series: World War II War Diaries, Other Operational Records

and Histories, National Archives Catalog, https://catalog.archives.gov/id/78321569; USS *QUINCY*—War Diary, 4/1-30/44, Record Group 38: Records of the Office of the Chief of Naval Operations, Series: World War II War Diaries, Other Operational Records and Histories, National Archives Catalog, https://catalog.archives.gov/id/78422739; USS *QUINCY*—War Diary, 10/1-31/44, Record Group 38: Records of the Office of the Chief of Naval Operations, Series: World War II War Diaries, Other Operational Records and Histories, National Archives Catalog, https://catalog.archives.gov/id/78647339; USS *QUINCY*—War Diary, 9/1-30/44, Record Group 38: Records of the Office of the Chief of Naval Operations, Series: World War II War Diaries, Other Operational Records and Histories, National Archives Catalog, https://catalog.archives.gov/id/139736554; USS *QUINCY*—War Diary, 10/1-31/45, Record Group 38: Records of the Office of the Chief of Naval Operations, Series: World War II War Diaries, Other Operational Records and Histories, National Archives Catalog, https://catalog.archives.gov/id/77593714; USS *QUINCY*—War Diary, 11/1-30/45, Record Group 38: Records of the Office of the Chief of Naval Operations, Series: World War II War Diaries, Other Operational Records and Histories, National Archives Catalog, https://catalog.archives.gov/id/77572848; USS *QUINCY*—War Diary, 2/1-28/45, Record Group 38: Records of the Office of the Chief of Naval Operations, Series: World War II War Diaries, Other Operational Records and Histories, https://catalog.archives.gov/id/139885913; USS *QUINCY*—War Diary, 8/1-31/44, Record Group 38: Records of the Office of the Chief of Naval Operations, Series: World War II War Diaries, Other Operational Records and Histories, National Archives Catalog, https://catalog.archives.gov/id/78621763; USS *QUINCY*—War Diary, 6/1-30/44, Record Group 38: Records of the Office of the Chief of Naval Operations, Series: World War II War Diaries, Other Operational Records and Histories, National Archives Catalog, https://catalog.archives.gov/id/78513181; USS *QUINCY*—War Diary, 11/1-30/44, Record Group 38: Records of the Office of the Chief of Naval Operations, Series: World War II War Diaries, Other Operational Records and Histories, National Archives Catalog, https://catalog.archives.gov/id/78708829; USS *Quincy* (CA-71), Naval History and Heritage Command, https://www.history.navy.mil/our-collections/photography/us-navy-ships/alphabetical-listing/q/uss-quincy--ca-71-.html.

[6]Erin Blakemore, "How PTSD Went from 'Shell-Shock' to a Recognized Medical Diagnosis," *National Geographic,* June 16, 2020, https://www.nationalgeographic.com/history/article/ptsd-shell-shock-to-recognized-medical-diagnosis.

[7]"The Election of 1800-1801," History-Founders, The Lehrman Institute, https://lehrmaninstitute.org/history/1800.html.

[8]"John Quincy Adams and His Struggle Against Slavery and the Gag Rule—Handout A: Narrative," Bill of Rights Institute, https://billofrightsinstitute.org/activities/john-quincy-adams-and-his-struggle-against-slavery-and-the-gag-rule-handout-a-narrative.

[9]AZ Quotes, https://www.azquotes.com/quote/1308563#google_vignette.

[10] "Thomas Jefferson (13/04/1743-04/07/1826), American Politician," Busca Biografías, https://www.buscabiografias.com/biografia/verDetalle/2704/Thomas%20Jefferson.

[11] "Jefferson, Thomas, and the Practice of Law," Encyclopedia Virginia, Virginia Humanities, https://encyclopediavirginia.org/entries/jefferson-thomas-and-the-practice-of-law/.

[12] Trevor English, "7 things invented or popularized by Thomas Jefferson, Interesting Engineering, July 20, 2023, https://interestingengineering.com/lists/7-things-you-wont-believe-thomas-jefferson-invented.

[13] History.com Editors, "Sally Hemings," January 28, 2010, updated July 11, 2023, https://www.history.com/topics/slavery/sally-hemings.

[14] "People and Ideas: Thomas Jefferson," Frontline, PBS, https://www.pbs.org/wgbh/pages/frontline/godinamerica/people/thomas-jefferson.html.

[15] "Jefferson's Attitudes towards Slavery," Monticello, Thomas Jefferson Foundation, https://www.monticello.org/thomas-jefferson/jefferson-slavery/jefferson-s-attitudes-toward-slavery/.

[16] Jon Meacham, *Thomas Jefferson: The Art of Power* (New York: Random House, 2012), 478, 479.

[17] Wolf by the Ear (quotation), Research and Education, Thomas Jefferson Encyclopedia, Monticello, Thomas Jefferson Foundation, https://www.monticello.org/research-education/thomas-jefferson-encyclopedia/wolf-ear-quotation/.

[18] The Practice of Slavery at Monticello, Thomas Jefferson, Jefferson and Slavery, Monticello, Thomas Jefferson Foundation, https://www.monticello.org/thomas-jefferson/jefferson-slavery/the-practice-of-slavery-at-monticello/.

[19] Greg Timmons, "How Slavery Became the Economic Engine of the South," History, March 6, 2018, updated April 2, 2024, https://www.history.com/news/slavery-profitable-southern-economy; Dinesh D'Souza, "We the Slave Owners," Hoover Institution, September 1, 1995, https://www.hoover.org/research/we-slave-owners; "There Were 4 Million Enslaved Peopled Counted in the 186o Census. That Dropped to Zero in the 1870 Count," USA Facts, https://usafacts.org/articles/the-1860-census-counted-4-million-enslaved-people-it-counted-zero-in-1870/#:~:text=In%201860%2C%20the%20government%20counted,slaves%20in%20Confederate%20states%20free.

[20] Henry Wiencek, "The Dark Side of Thomas Jefferson," *Smithsonian Magazine*, October 2012, https://www.smithsonianmag.com/history/the-dark-side-of-thomas-jefferson-35976004/.

[21] John F. Kennedy, "Remarks at a Dinner Honoring Nobel Prize Winners of the Western Hemisphere," April 29, 1962, The American Presidency Project, UC Santa Barbara, https://www.presidency.ucsb.edu/documents/remarks-dinner-honoring-nobel-prize-winners-the-western-hemisphere.

[22] John F. Kennedy's 1963 Televised Address to the Nation on Civil Rights, John F. Kennedy Library Foundation, YouTube, https://www.youtube.com/watch?v=58O2De-iPOk.

[23] Billal Rahman, "Video Shows Moment Laken Riley's Family Find Out About Murder," https://www.msn.com/en-us/news/crime/video-shows-moment-laken-rileys-family-find-out-about-murder/ar-AA1uuKoQ.

[24] "Alicia Ostriker Reads and Discusses Emma Lazarus' 'The New Colossus,'" Programs, Poetry & Literature, Audio Recordings, Poetry of America, Library of Congress, https://www.loc.gov/programs/poetry-and-literature/audio-recordings/poetry-of-america/item/poetry-00001033/alicia-ostriker-emma-lazarus/; "Emma Lazarus," Women of Valor, Sharing Stories, Inspiring Change, Jewish Women's Archive, https://jwa.org/womenofvalor/lazarus.

[25] Adam E. Zielinski, "The Election of 1800: Adams vs. Jefferson," American Battlefield Trust, May 20, 2020, updated November 29, 2023, https://www.battlefields.org/learn/articles/election-1800-adams-vs-jefferson.

[26] Thomas Jefferson to John Adams, 28 October 1813, Founders Online, National Archives, revolution.https://founders.archives.gov/documents/Jefferson/03-06-02-0446.

[27] "Presidential Orders upon the Death of a President," The American Presidency Project, December 5, 2018, UC Santa Barbara, https://www.presidency.ucsb.edu/analyses/presidential-orders-upon-the-death-president.

[28] Michael S. Rosenwald, "John Adams Was Buried Days before His Son, President John Quincy Adams, Knew He Was Dead," *Telegram & Gazette*, December 8, 2018, https://www.telegram.com/story/news/nation-world/2018/12/08/john-adams-was-buried-days-before-his-son-president-john-quincy-adams-knew-he-was-dead/6745179007/.

[29] History.com Editors, "Abigail Adams," History, https://www.history.com/topics/first-ladies/abigail-adams.

[30] "John Quincy Adams, July 11, 1767-February 23, 1848," American History Central, https://www.whitehouse.gov/about-the-white-house/presidents/john-quincy-adams/ https://www.americanhistorycentral.com/entries/john-quincy-adams/; "John Quincy Adams," Britannica, https://www.britannica.com/biography/John-Quincy-Adams.

[31] "Cicero and the Constitution," National Constitution Center, November 18, 2022, https://constitutioncenter.org/media/files/Cicero_and_the_Constitution_Transcript.pdf.

[32] Maris Fessenden, "John Quincy Adams Was an Ardent Supporter of Exploration," Smithsonian Magazine, May 2015, https://www.smithsonianmag.com/smart-news/john-quincy-adams-ardent-supporter-exploration-180955203/.

[33] "John Quincy Adams and the Gag Rule," Bill of Rights Institute, https://www.billofrightsinstitute.org/essays/john-quincy-adams-and-the-gag-rule.

[34] History.com Editors, "Panama Canal," History, https://www.history.com/topics/landmarks/panama-canal.

[35] History.com Editors, "Theodore Roosevelt," U.S. Presidents, History, https://www.history.com/topics/us-presidents/theodore-roosevelt#theodore-roosevelt-s-early-life-and-career; "Roosevelt's Tiffany Bowie Knife," Teddy Roosevelt Live, October 24, 2014, https://teddyrooseveltlive.com/2014/10/24/roosevelts-tiffany-bowie-knife/.

[36]"Theodore Roosevelt and Conservation," Theodore Roosevelt, National Park North Dakota, National Park Service, https://www.nps.gov/thro/learn/historyculture/theodore-roosevelt-and-conservation.htm.
[37]"Theodore Roosevelt and Conservation," National Park Service, https://www.nps.gov/thro/learn/historyculture/theodore-roosevelt-and-conservation.htm.
[38]"Theodore Roosevelt and Conservation."
[39]"1506: Christopher Columbus Dies," This Day in History, History, https://www.history.com/this-day-in-history/christopher-columbus-dies; "Christopher Columbus," Britannica, https://www.britannica.com/biography/Christopher-Columbus.
[40]Kevin Gover, "Nation to Nation: Treaties between the United States and American Indian Nations," American Indian, Summer/Fall 2014, https://www.americanindianmagazine.org/story/nation-nation-treaties-between-united-states-and-american-indian-nations.
[41]Sitting Bull, AZ Quotes, https://www.azquotes.com/author/2148-Sitting_Bull.
[42]Finis Dunaway, "The 'Crying Indian' Ad that Fooled the Environmental Movement, *Chicago Tribune*, June 24, 2024, https://www.chicagotribune.com/2017/11/21/the-crying-indian-ad-that-fooled-the-environmental-movement/.
[43]Ben Marks, "Stuck on Colorforms, the Two-dimensional Toy Beloved By Mid-century Modern Kids," Collectors Weekly, May 16, 2014, https://www.collectorsweekly.com/articles/colorforms-the-two-dimensional-toy-for-mid-century-modern-kids/.
[44]"List of Indian Reservations in the United States," Wikipedia, https://en.wikipedia.org/wiki/List_of_Indian_reservations_in_the_United_States.
[45]David Treuer, "Coping with Life on Indian Reservations Today," Native America Today, https://americanindiancoc.org/coping-with-life-on-indian-reservations-today/; "Understanding the Realties of Reservation Life," Native Hope, November 21, 2019, https://blog.nativehope.org/understanding-the-realities-of-reservation-life.
[46]"Introductory Segment from Kennedy Library & Museum Rededication Film (1993)," About Us, About the JFK Library, Fast Facts about the John F. Kennedy Presidential Library & Museum, John F. Kennedy Presidential Library & Museum, https://www.jfklibrary.org/about-us/about-the-jfk-library/kennedy-library-fast-facts/rededication-film-intro.
[47]"What Would the USA Look Like if Robert F. Kennedy Wasn't Assassinated?," "RFK: America's Lost President," DocuBay, https://www.youtube.com/watch?v=yJhGDRs9KRc.
[48]"Robert Francis Kennedy," The Kennedy Family, About JFK, Learn, John F. Kennedy Presidential Library & Museum, https://www.jfklibrary.org/learn/about-jfk/the-kennedy-family/robert-f-kennedy.
[49]Rick Hampson, "RFK's Visit to Appalachia, 50 Years Later: How Kennedy Country Became Trump Country," *USA Today*, February 12, 2018, https://www.usatoday.com/story/news/politics/2018/02/12/rfks-visit-appalachia-50-years-later-how-kennedy-country-became-trump-country/310267002/.

⁵⁰Tina Rodia, "Fifty years ago, RFK's speech at The Palestra on Vietnam," Penn Today, June 5, 2018, https://penntoday.upenn.edu/news/fifty-years-ago-rfks-speech-palestra-vietnam.

⁵¹Chris Matthews, *Bobby Kennedy: A Raging Spirit* (New York: Simon & Schuster, 2017), 24.

⁵²The Papers of Robert F. Kennedy, Senate Papers, Speeches and Press Releases, Box 4, "4/1/68–4/10/68," John F. Kennedy Presidential Library.

⁵³History.com Editors, "Robert Kennedy," History, November 9, 2009, Updated August 18, 2018, https://www.history.com/topics/1960s/robert-f-kennedy.

⁵⁴Larry Tye, *Robert Kennedy, The Making of a Liberal Lion* (New York: Random House, 2016), 444.

⁵⁵Garrett M. Graff, *Watergate: A New History* (Avid Reader Press/Simon & Schuster, 2022), 95.

⁵⁶"I Want the Brookings Institute Safe Cleaned Out," The Secret White House Tapes, The Presidency, Miller Center, UVA, https://millercenter.org/the-presidency/secret-white-house-tapes/i-want-brookings-institute-safe-cleaned-out.

⁵⁷Stephen Robertson, "New York Times Co. v. United States (1971)," Free Speech Center at Middle Tennessee State University, https://firstamendment.mtsu.edu/article/new-york-times-co-v-united-states/; Ron Elving, "History-making Whistleblower Daniel Ellsberg Has Died at 92," All Things Considered, NPR, June 16, 2023, https://www.npr.org/2023/06/16/1162158609/daniel-ellsberg-obituary-pentagon-papers.

⁵⁸John A. Farrell, *Richard Nixon: The Life* (New York: Vintage, 2017), 343.

⁵⁹"The Chennault Affair," LBJ Presidential Library, https://www.lbjlibrary.org/media-kit/chennault-affair.

⁶⁰Farrell, *Richard Nixon: The Life*, 343.

⁶¹"187. Telephone Conversation between President Johnson and Richard Nixon," Foreign Relations of the United States, 1964–1968, Volume 7, Vietnam, September 1968–January 1969, Office of the Historian, Department of State, Https://History.State.Gov/Historicaldocuments/Frus1964-68v07/D187.

⁶²"Vietnam War—Johnson Peace Process "Chennault Affair—"Nixon's October Surprise" Documents, Access History, BACM Research, PaperlessArchives.com, https://downloads.paperlessarchives.com/p/ysge/.

⁶³"What is the Logan Act?" BBC News, February 14, 2017, https://www.bbc.com/news/world-us-canada-38973965.

⁶⁴Farrell, *Richard Nixon: The Life*, 343.

⁶⁵ Farrell, *Richard Nixon: The Life*, 57.

⁶⁶Jennifer Rosenberg, "Biography of Richard Nixon, 37th President of the United States," May 19, 2019, Thought.co, https://www.thoughtco.com/richard-nixon-fast-facts-104880.

⁶⁷Farrell, *Richard Nixon: The Life*, Chapter 10, "Checkers."

⁶⁸Farrell, *Richard Nixon: The Life*, 57.

⁶⁹History.com Editors, "Richard M. Nixon," History, https://www.history.com/topics/us-presidents/richard-m-nixon.

[70]"Nixon's Checkers Speech," American Experience, PBS, September 23, 1952, https://www.pbs.org/wgbh/americanexperience/features/eisenhower-checkers/.
[71]"Richard Nixon: 'You Don't Have Nixon to Kick around any More,'" https://vimeo.com/225273702.
[72]"New Revelations from the Nixon Tapes," Sunday Morning, CBS News, https://www.cbsnews.com/news/new-revelations-from-the-nixon-tapes/.
[73]"Richard Nixon's Top Domestic and Foreign Policy Achievements," Richard Nixon Foundation, https://www.nixonfoundation.org/richard-nixons-top-domestic-and-foreign-policy-achievements/.
[74]"Richard Nixon on Nightline with Ted Koppel," Full Interview, January 7, 1992, YouTube, https://www.youtube.com/watch?v=iWPwT6DPrDw.
[75]Richard Nixon, *Leaders* (Brentwood, TN: Warner Books, 1982), 322.
[76]Roger Baylor, "Hunter S. Thompson Eulogizes Richard M. Nixon (1994): 'He Was a Crook,'" January 14, 2022, https://www.rogerbaylor.com/2022/01/14/hunter-s-thompson-eulogizes-richard-m-nixon-1994-he-was-a-crook/.
[77]Bill Chappell, "Derek Chauvin Is Sentenced To 22 1/2 Years For George Floyd's Murder," NPR, June 25, 2021, https://www.npr.org/sections/trial-over-killing-of-george-floyd/2021/06/25/1009524284/derek-chauvin-sentencing-george-floyd-murder.
[78]Brad Polumbo, "George Floyd Riots Caused Record-Setting $2 Billion in Damage, New Report Says. Here's Why the True Cost Is Even Higher," Foundation for Economic Education, https://fee.org/articles/george-floyd-riots-caused-record-setting-2-billion-in-damage-new-report-says-here-s-why-the-true-cost-is-even-higher/.
[79]Javote Anderson, "Martin Luther King Jr.'s Words of Unity and Truth Transcend How They Are Often Twisted," USA Today, January 14, 2022, https://www.usatoday.com/story/news/nation/2022/01/14/mlk-day-quotes-words-unity/6526355001/.
[80]"Martin Luther King, Jr. Was Arrested 29 Times for These So-called Crimes," Black History, https://www.blackhistory.com/2019/11/martin-luther-king-jr-was-arrested-29-times-crimes.html.
[81]"Martin Luther King, Jr. Quotes about Hate," AZ Quotes, https://www.azquotes.com/author/8044-Martin_Luther King Jr./tag/hate#google_vignette.
[82]revcowboybabybearpoom,"The Filmography of Ronald Reagan," IMDB, https://www.imdb.com/list/ls505473144/.
[83]"Presidential Historians Survey 2021," C-Span, https://www.c-span.org/presidentsurvey2021/?page=overall.

84"Top Ten Achievements of Ronald Reagan's Presidency," Reagan.com, October 18, 2017, https://www.reagan.com/top-ten-achievements-of-ronald-reagans-presidency.
85Ronald Reagan, "Republican National Convention Speech 1976," August 19, 1976, Ronald Reagan Presidential Library & Museum, https://www.reaganlibrary.gov/archives/speech/republican-national-convention-speech-1976.
86Peggy Noonan, *When Character Was King: A Story of Ronald Reagan* (New York: Penguin Books, 2002), 20–23.
87Bill O'Reilly and Martin Dugard, *Killing Reagan: The Violent Assault That Changed a Presidency* (New York: Henry Holt and Co., 2015, 177–180; Noonan, *When Character Was King*, 185, 195.
88Ronald Reagan, "Message to the Congress on Energy Security," May 6, 1987, Ronald Reagan Presidential Library & Museum, https://www.reaganlibrary.gov/archives/speech/message-congress-energy-security; Tom Murse, "A Brief History of White House Solar Panels," Thought.co, August 3, 2021, https://www.thoughtco.com/history-of-white-house-solar-panels-3322255.
89"Ronald Reagan Fires 11,359 Air-traffic Controllers," This Day in History, History, https://www.history.com/this-day-in-history/reagan-fires-11359-air-traffic-controllers.
90O'Reilly and Dugard, *Killing Reagan*, 252; History.com Editors, "Iran-Contra Affair," History, August 10, 2017, updated January 17, 2020, https://www.history.com/topics/1980s/iran-contra-affair.
91Ronald Reagan, "Radio Address to the Nation on Prayer," September 18, 1982, Ronald Reagan Presidential Library & Museum, https://www.reaganlibrary.gov/archives/speech/radio-address-nation-prayer.
92Ronald Reagan, "Radio Address to the Nation on Flag Day and Father's Day," Ronald Reagan Presidential Library & Museum, June 14, 1986, https://www.reaganlibrary.gov/archives/speech/radio-address-nation-flag-day-and-fathers-day.
93"President Reagan Challenges Gorbachev to 'Tear Down This Wall," This Day in History, History, https://www.history.com/this-day-in-history/reagan-challenges-gorbachev-to-tear-down-the-berlin-wall; Peter Robinson, "'Tear Down This Wall': How Top Advisers Opposed Reagan's Challenge to Gorbachev—But Lost," *Prologue Magazine* 39, no. 2 (Summer 2007), https://www.archives.gov/publications/prologue/2007/summer/berlin.html.
94Nikolay Sevchenoko,"Did Reagan Really Coin the Term 'Trust but verify,' a Proverb Revived by HBO's Chernobyl?" Russia Beyond, June 17, 2019, https://www.rbth.com/lifestyle/330521-reagan-trust-but-verify-chernobyl.
95Ronald Reagan, "Inaugural Address 1981," Ronald Reagan Presidential Library & Museum, https://www.reaganlibrary.gov/archives/speech/inaugural-address-1981.
96George Washington, Quotes, George Washington's Mount Vernon, https://www.mountvernon.org/library/digitalhistory/past-projects/quotes/article/however-political-parties-may-now-and-then-answer-popular-ends-they-are-likely-in-the-course-of-time-and-things-to-become-potent-engines-by-which-cunning-ambitious-and-

unprincipled-men-will-be-enabled-to-subvert-the-power-of-the-people-and-to-usurp-for-th.

[97] Ronald Reagan, "January 5, 1967: Inaugural Address (Public Ceremony)," Ronald Reagan Presidential Library & Museum, https://www.reaganlibrary.gov/archives/speech/january-5-1967-inaugural-address-public-ceremony.

[98] Ronald Reagan, "Farewell Address to the Nation," January 11, 1989, Ronald Reagan Presidential Library & Museum, https://www.reaganlibrary.gov/archives/speech/farewell-address-nation.

[99] Epictetus, AZ Quotes, https://www.azquotes.com/author/4528-Epictetus.

[100] Greg Keraghorsian, "'That Was a Lark': A War Hero from Stanford and His Tragic VP Debate in 1992," SFGate, August 11, 2020, https://www.sfgate.com/politics/article/Stockdale-Stanford-vice-president-debate-1992-15427467.php.

[101] Sharon Lebell, *The Manual for Living—Epictetus: A New Interpretation* (New York: HarperCollins, 1995), 7–8.

[102] James B. Stockdale, *Courage under Fire: Testing Epictetus's Doctrines in a Laboratory of Human Behavior* (Stanford, CA: Hoover Institution Press, 1993), 7.

[103] Katie Lang, "Medal of Honor Monday: Navy Vice Adm. James Stockdale," DOD News, Department of Defense, March 2, 2020, https://www.defense.gov/News/Feature-Stories/Story/article/2097870/.

[104] Stockdale, *Courage under Fire*, 5; "James B. Stockdale, Politician, Class of 1947, " Notable Graduates, United States Naval Academy, https://www.usna.edu/Notables/featured/10stockdale.php.

[105] George Spencer, "Strength in Unity," Courage 101: True Tales of Grit & Glory, George Spencer Substack, March 14, 2022, https://georgespencer.substack.com/p/xxx.

[106] David A. Cox, "Return with Honor, February 24, 2016, America's Navy, https://www.navy.mil/Press-Office/News-Stories/Article/2260480/.

[107] "James Bond Stockdale, Vice Admiral, U.S. Navy, World War II, Korea, Vietnam, Prisoner of War 9 Sep 1965–12 Feb 1973," Mt. Soledad National Veterans Memorial, https://soledadmemorial.org/plaques/vice-admiral-james-bond-stockdale.

[108] "Former POWs," We Honor Veterans, https://www.wehonorveterans.org/working-for-veterans/by-population/former-pows/#:~:text=More%20than%20one%2Dhalf%20million,War%20 since%20the%20 American%20Revolution.

[109] "Vietnam War U.S. Military Fatal Casualty Statistics," Military Records, National Archives, https://www.archives.gov/research/military/vietnam-war/casualty-statistics.

[110] "'You've got to find what you love,' Jobs says," Stanford Report, Stanford University, June 12, 2005, https://news.stanford.edu/stories/2005/06/youve-got-find-love-jobs-says.

[111] "Inside the Lockheed Martin Laser Technology," August 11, 2022, Lockheed Martin, https://www.lockheedmartin.com/en-us/news/features/2022/inside-the-lockheed-martin-laser-technology-that-defeated-a-surrogate-cruise-missile.html.

[112] "Redefining the Boundaries of Human Capabilities Requires Pioneers," Neuralink, https://neuralink.com/.
[113] Sarah Pruitt, "Ted Kennedy's Chappaquiddick Incident: What Really Happened," *History*, September 8, 2018,
 https://www.history.com/news/ted-kennedy-chappaquiddick-incident-what-really-happened-facts.
[114] John Uri, "60 Years Ago: President Kennedy Reaffirms Moon-Landing Goal in Rice University Speech," *Roundup Reads*, NASA, https://roundupreads.jsc.nasa.gov/roundup/2002/60%20Years%20Ago%20President%20Kennedy%20Reaffirms%20MoonLanding%20Goal%20in%20Rice%20University%20Speech.
[115] Amie Parnes, "Next Step Not Clear for Vicki Kennedy," *Politico*, August 29, 2009.
[116] Ari Shapiro, "Romney's 1994 Senate Loss Left Lasting Marks," NPR, May 7, 2012, https://www.npr.org/2012/05/07/152056667/romneys-1994-senate-loss-left-lasting-marks.
[117] Edward M. Kennedy, *True Compass: A Memoir* (New York: Twelve, 2009), 292.
[118] Neetal Parekh, "Senator Ted Kennedy's Legislative Legacy," *Find Law*, March 21, 2019, https://www.findlaw.com/legalblogs/law-and-life/senator-ted-kennedys-legislative-legacy/
[119] James Martin, S. J., "Kennedy's Letter to Benedict, and Reply," *America The Jesuit Review*, August 30, 2009,
 https://www.americamagazine.org/content/all-things/kennedys-letter-benedict-and-reply.
[120] Kaleena Fraga, "Meet Gladys Presley, Elvis Presley's Mother and The 'Love of His Life,'" All Things Interesting, January 13, 2022, updated June 16, 2024, https://allthatsinteresting.com/gladys-presley.
[121] Robert Yaniz, Jr., "Elvis Presley Always Wondered What His Life Would've Been Like if His Stillborn Twin Brother Survived, Showbiz Cheatsheet, September 30, 2022, https://www.cheatsheet.com/entertainment/elvis-presley-always-wondered-life-if-stillborn-twin-brother-survived.html/.
[122] "Achievements," Biography, About Elvis, Graceland, https://www.graceland.com/achievements.
[123] Jael Rucker, "A Guide to All 31 Elvis Presley Movies in Order and Where to Watch in 2023," One 37 PM, October 9, 2023,
 https://www.one37pm.com/popular-culture/a-guide-to-all-31-elvis-presley-movies-in-order.
[124] Duke Haddad, ED.D., "The Philanthropic Side of Elvis Presley," Pay It Forward, NonProfit Pro, November 3, 2017, https://www.nonprofitpro.com/post/philanthropic-side-elvis-presley/.

[125] Robert Morrison, "If I Can Dream: The Elvis Tribute to Martin Luther King, Jr.," The Conversation, March 29, 2018, https://theconversation.com/if-i-can-dream-the-elvis-tribute-to-martin-luther-king-jr-87845; Caleb Shumate, "'If I Can Dream'": Elvis' Cultural Contributions to Civil Rights," The Libertarian Republic, https://thelibertarianrepublic.com/elvis-cultural-contributions-to-civil-rights/.

[126] Josh Sims, "Elvis Presley: The King of Fashion," Fashionbeans, December 3, 2024, https://www.fashionbeans.com/article/elvis-presley-fashion/; Elvis Presley, "Unchained Melody," https://www.youtube.com/watch?v=61-RycNKdJk.

[127] "1959: Buddy Holly, Richie Valens and 'The Big Bopper' Die in a Plane Crash," This Day in History, History, https://www.history.com/this-day-in-history/the-day-the-music-died.

[128] George Simpson, "Elvis Presley: The Book King Was Reading when He Died on the Toilet upstairs at Graceland," Express, March 11, 2022, https://www.express.co.uk/entertainment/music/1578862/Elvis-Presley-book-reading-when-died-toilet-Graceland-upstairs.

[129] "Statement by the President on the Death of Elvis Presley," August 17, 1977, The American Presidency Project, UC Santa Barbara, https://www.presidency.ucsb.edu/documents/statement-the-president-the-death-elvis-presley.

[130] Stefan Kyriazis, "Frank Sinatra Blasted 'Degenerate' Elvis as a 'Cretinous Goon' but Later Tried to Save Him," Express, December 4, 2021, updated December 6, 2021, https://www.express.co.uk/entertainment/music/1531495/Frank-Sinatra-Elvis-Presley-music-friends-death-Old-Blue-Eyes-The-King.

[131] Jerry Schilling and Chuck Crisafu, *Me and a Guy Named Elvis: My Lifelong Friendship with Elvis Presley* (Garden City Park, NY: Avery Publishing Group, 2006), 324–325; Robert Fontenot, "The Funeral of the King of Rock and Rock," Liveabout, December 28, 2018, https://www.liveabout.com/details-of-elvis-presleys-funeral-2522426.

[132] DAILYMAIL.COM REPORTER, "'Reading Those Truths Tore Him Apart': A Tell-all Book written by Elvis Presley's Bodyguards about His Drug Addiction 'Pushed Him over the Edge' Just Days before His Death," Daily Mail, August 16, 2017, https://www.dailymail.co.uk/news/article-4794622/Elvis-pushed-edge-bodyguards-tell-book.html; Alan Hanson, "'Elvis: What Happened?' Not the Best Elvis Biography, but a Historic One," Elvis History Blog, April 2008, http://www.elvis-history-blog.com/elvis_biography.html.

[133] Brianne Tracy, "Lisa Marie Presley Reveals in Posthumous Memoir She Was 'Always Worried' about Dad Elvis 'Dying' (Exclusive)," People, September 26, 2024, https://people.com/lisa-marie-presley-was-worried-about-dad-elvis-dying-memoir-exclusive-8718495; Biography.com Editors, "Lisa Marie Presley," Biography, October 8, 2024, https://www.biography.com/celebrities/lisa-marie-presley; Olivia Munson, "How Did Elvis Presley Die? A Look inside the Rock Legend's Death and Health," USA Today, September 19, 2022, updated February 23, 2024, https://www.usatoday.com/story/entertainment/celebrities/2022/09/19/how-did-elvis-presley-die/7930846001/.

[134] Kristina Robb-Dover, "The 10 Drugs that Were in Elvis Presley's System When He Overdosed—and Other Revelations," FHE Health, April 20, 2024, https://fherehab.com/learning/elvis-presley-drugs-led-to-overdose; "Medical Examiner's Report on the Death of Elvis (1977)," Preslaw, https://preslaw.info/medical-examiners-report-autopsy-on-the-death-of-elvis-presley.

[135] Jennifer Mathews, "The Sandwich Elvis Presley Loved So Much, He Ate It by the Loaf," Food Republic, April 25, 2025, https://www.foodrepublic.com/1568366/elvis-presley-favorite-sandwich/.

[136] Sara Traynor, "Elvis Presley's Disturbing Diet—You Won't Believe What He Ate," So Yummy!, May 29, 2024, https://soyummy.com/entertaining/elvis-presley-diet/.

[137] "The Artist and the Businessman: Elvis Presley Meets Col. Tom Parker," The Official Blog of Graceland, February 5, 2016, Graceland, https://www.graceland.com/blog/posts/the-artist-and-the-businessman-elvis-presley-meets-col-tom-parker.

[138] Matt Friedlander, "The King's Final Act: Remembering the Last Song Elvis Presley Ever Played on Stage, American Songwriter, June 26, 2024, https://americansongwriter.com/the-kings-final-act-remembering-the-last-song-elvis-presley-ever-played-on-stage/; Skyler Caruso, "Elvis Presley's Death: The Details Behind the King of Rock 'n' Roll's Passing," People, June 13, 2024, https://people.com/music/elvis-presley-death-everything-to-know/; Susan Doll, Elvis Presley Biography, How Stuff Works, https://entertainment.howstuffworks.com/elvis-presley-biography35.htm.

[139] George Simpson, "Elvis Presley's abundant generosity: 'I thought he was going to pass out, he was shaking,'" Express, November 29, 2022, https://www.express.co.uk/entertainment/music/1703134/Elvis-Presley-generosity-Elvis-cousin.

[140] Rich Tucker, "America's Debt, Through the Eyes of the Founders," The Heritage Foundation, October 8, 2013, https://www.heritage.org/political-process/report/americas-debt-through-the-eyes-the-founders.

[141] "Washington's Farewell Address to the People of the United States," SENATE DOCUMENT NO. 106–21 (Washington, DC: Government Printing Office, 2000), https://www.govinfo.gov/content/pkg/GPO-CDOC-106sdoc21/pdf/GPO-CDOC-106sdoc21.pdf.

[142]Michelle Fox, "The U.S. National Debt Is Rising by $1 Trillion about Every 100 Days," CNBC, March 1, 2024, updated March 4, 2024, https://www.cnbc.com/2024/03/01/the-us-national-debt-is-rising-by-1-trillion-about-every-100-days.html.

[143]Les Rubin, "America Beware, Our Spending and Debt Is Leading Us to Failure," https://www.google.com/search?client=safari&rls=en&q=MainstreetEconomics.org&ie=UTF-8&oe=UTF

[144]Victoria Guida, "Fed's Powell: 'Urgent' for US to focus on debt sustainability," Politico, February 4, 2024, https://www.politico.com/news/2024/02/04/fed-powell-debt-sustainability-00139528.

[145]Vishesh Raisinghani, "'Concerning': Hedge Fund Manager Bill Ackman Reacts to Historian's Warning about the Brewing U.S. Debt Crisis," Yahoo! Finance, July 11, 2024, https://finance.yahoo.com/news/concerning-hedge-fund-manager-bill-105000702.html.

[146]Frederick Hernandez, "Why the National Debt Matters for National Security," Bipartisan Policy Center, November 14, 2024, https://bipartisanpolicy.org/explainer/why-the-national-debt-matters-for-national-security/.

[147]Adrian Volenik, "'Nobody Had Any Mondy. The Rich People Didn't Have Any Mondy,' Said Charlie Munger about the Great Depression—'It's Been Very Helpful to Me,'" Yahoo! Finance, August 2, 2024, https://finance.yahoo.com/news/nobody-had-money-rich-people-163122312.html.

[148]Rob Kelley, "The Top 4 Charlie Munger Speeches, Interviews and Documentaries," The Daily Doc, December 1, 2023, https://dailydoc.com/best-charlie-munger-speeches-and-interviews/; Frank Holmes, "How Losing An Eye Helped Charlie Munger See Success," Forbes, December 4, 2023, https://www.forbes.com/sites/greatspeculations/2023/12/04/how-losing-an-eye-helped-charlie-munger-see-success/.

[149]Nicole Goodkind and Eva Rothenberg, "Warren Buffett Holds First Berkshire Hathaway Meeting without Charlie Munger, CNN, May 4, 2024, https://www.cnn.com/2024/05/04/investing/berkshire-hathaway-meeting/index.html#:~:text=The%20pair%20first%20met%20in,a%20sage%20price%20of%20advice.

[150]Theron Mohamed, "Charlie Munger Was a Fraction as Wealthy as Warren Buffett. He Would've Been Worth over $10 Billion if He'd Kept All of His Berkshire Hathway Stock," Yahoo! Finance, November 28, 2023, https://finance.yahoo.com/news/charlie-munger-fraction-wealthy-warren-183501213.html.

[151]Abi Bus, "Charlie Munger: Role, Investment Philosophy, and Berkshire's 'Four Giants,'" Supermoney, April 30, 2024, https://www.supermoney.com/encyclopedia/charlie-munger.

[152]"How Charlie Munger Uses Inversion Thinking Process in Life," Daily Journal 2020, https://www.youtube.com/watch?v=tcq6ZyfQV2w.

[153] Thomas Waschenfelder, "Circle of Competence: Charlie Munger and Warren Buffett's Greatest Secret," Wealest, May 13, 2023, https://www.wealest.com/articles/circle-of-competence?format=amp.

[154] Maria Di Mento, "Charlie Munger, Big Donor and Warren Buffett's Business Partner, Has Died, Philanthropy, November 28, 2023, https://www.philanthropy.com/article/charlie-munger-big-donor-and-warren-buffetts-business-partner-has-died.

[155] Chris Clark, "'You Gotta Do It': The Late Charlie Munger Once Said Your First $100K is the Toughest to Earn—but Most Crucial to Building Wealth. Here Are 5 Ways to Reach That Magical Milestone," Yahoo! Finance, November 29, 2023 https://finance.yahoo.com/news/b-gotta-charlie-munger-says-140000516.html.

[156] Tom Huddleston, "At 99, Billionaire Charlie Munger Shared His No. 1 Tip for Living a Long, Happy Life: 'Avoid Crazy at All Costs,'" Make It, CNBC, December 3, 2023, https://www.cnbc.com/2023/12/03/charlie-munger-best-tip-for-long-life-avoid-crazy-at-all-costs.html.

[157] Huddleston, "At 99, Billionaire Charlie Munger Shared His No. 1 Tip for Living a Long, Happy Life: 'Avoid Crazy at All Costs.'"

[158] Johnny Hopkins, "14 Of Charlie Munger's Funniest Quotes," The Acquirer's Multiple, April 2, 2018, https://acquirersmultiple.com/2018/04/14-of-charlie-mungers-funniest-quotes/.

[159] Yun Li, "Charlie Munger Says Crypto Is a Bad Combo of Fraud and Delusion—'Good for Kidnappers,'" CNBC, November 15, 2022, https://www.cnbc.com/2022/11/15/charlie-munger-says-crypto-is-a-bad-combo-of-fraud-and-delusion-good-for-kidnappers.html.

[160] Quote Fancy, https://quotefancy.com/quote/1561883/Charlie-Munger-Go-to-bed-smarter-than-when-you-woke-up.

[161] Luke 1:26-38, God's Word Translation, Bible Gateway, https://www.biblegateway.com/passage/?search=Luke%201%3A26-38&version=GW.

[162] "Aleksandr Solzhenitsyn Quotes," Good Reads, https://www.goodreads.com/author/quotes/19771050.Aleksandr_Solzhenitsyn.

Made in United States
North Haven, CT
04 August 2025